THE CHURCH COMMUNITY IN CONTEMPORARY CULTURE

Evangelism and Engagement with Postmodern People

KIERAN BEVILLE

THE CHURCH COMMUNITY IN CONTEMPORARY CULTURE

Evangelism and Engagement with Postmodern People

Kieran Beville

Christian Publishing House

Cambridge, Ohio

Christian Publishing House

Professional Christian Publishing of the Good News

THE CHURCH COMMUNITY IN CONTEMPORARY CULTURE Evangelism and Engagement with Postmodern People

ISBN-13: 978-0692637685

ISBN-10: 0692637680

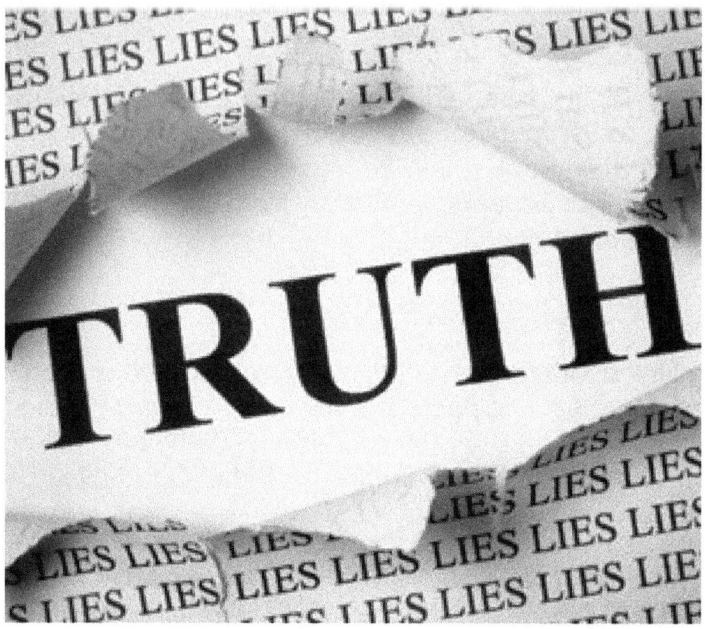

Table of Contents

Endorsements

Among its other strengths, this book is actually a good read, which I find to be a very pleasant surprise for a book on so complex a subject. It is also an important book because Postmodernism still plays a large role in our society, whether we continue to hear about it as a worldview or not. For a long time Christians used the term to refer to all that was evil in society, without really understanding what Postmodernism was ~ and is. Now, Beville takes us by the hand and guides us through a historical explanation of it, citing all the right spokespersons of the movement. Then, he explains to us how to relate to and reach Postmoderns on their own terms. In the process, he points out pitfalls for the church to avoid. I especially like his distinction between contextualization and syncretism: as Christians, we have to relate and be sensitive to Postmoderns without compromising our own belief system. The wealth of background material on Postmodernism in the book should be very helpful in differentiating the good from the bad in practice. Indeed, I can see Beville's book serving as an all-in-one manual or handbook for dealing with Postmodernism. That is quite an accomplishment for a book slightly over 200 pages, including a helpful bibliography for further reading on the subject.

Dr. Don Wilkins was the senior translator for the New American Standard Bible (NASB). He has a Th.M. in New Testament Languages from Talbot Seminary, Los Angeles, California and a Ph.D. from UCLA, in Classics. He also has a M.A. from UCLA and a M.Div. from Talbot. He has taught Greek at college level and beginning and intermediate level at Talbot, mostly college for about 20 years. Dr. Wilkins has worked in Bible research at The Lockman Foundation on and off since the early 1970s and has been Scholar in Residence there for 12 years.

INTRODUCTION

Once upon a time, Postmodernism was a buzzword. It was a new kind of belief system ~ though it would have rejected such a definition. It pronounced Modernism dead or at least in the throes of death. It was a wave that swept over the church promising to wash away sterile, dogmatic and outmoded forms of church. But whatever happened to postmodernism? Some regarded it as the start of an important historical transition from the modern era to something new, different, promising. It was hailed as a significant paradigm shift.

The 1960s saw widespread student anti-war, anti-establishment protests and the emergence of a counter-cultural hippie movement, rejecting traditional values. People began to critique Modernism and found it had not delivered the utopia it had promised and that it never could. The process of deconstruction moved outside the precincts of academia, and the idea that Modernism was an impoverished way of viewing the world became more popular.

New forms of art and architecture emerged which reflected a radical departure from conventional forms. Conceptual and installation art "evolved" and, I think, culminated in works like Tracy Emin's "Unmade Bed" with the detritus of contemporary life strewn on the floor. The nature of aesthetics had changed. Artists were ransacking, recycling, scavenging to present a latent form of Dadaism.[1] In literature, there was an insurrection against worn-out perceptions and a new postmodern perspective emerged.

---

[1] Dadaism was a form of artistic anarchy born out of disgust for the social, political and cultural values of the time (1916-1923). It embraced elements of art, music, poetry and theatre. Essentially it was a European avant-garde art movement that flouted conventional aesthetic and cultural values by producing works marked by nonsense, travesty, and incongruity.

2

As time went by Postmodernism become a more conventional than controversial theory and academics clashed about whether Modernism was a failed project or a project that needed reformation. The consensus view was that Modernism was kaput and it was a thorny question as to who was and was not Postmodern. By the end of the 1980s the terms were multiplying: post-Postmodernism, Supermodernism, Hypermodernism, Neo-modernism, Anti-modernism, Altermodernism.

During the 1990s, Postmodernism got swallowed whole by all the things it had spawned: multicultural art, feminist projects, politicized photo-works, and installations about gender, race, ethnicity, etc.

The Victoria and Albert Museum in London hosted a major design exhibition (24 September 2011 - 15 January 2012). This was the first in-depth survey of art, design and architecture of the 1970s and 1980s, examining one of the most contentious phenomena in recent art and design history. It showed how postmodernism evolved from a provocative architectural movement in the early 1970s (ignoring postmodern philosophy and literary criticism which predates the 1970s) and rapidly went on to influence all areas of popular culture including art, film, music, graphics and fashion.

What this exhibition unintentionally conveyed is that the subversive movement, which had seemed to be an earth-shattering, paradigm-shifting movement, was now categorized as just another trend, like Hippies, Punk or Goth. For this reason, many people think Postmodernism has disappeared.

At the outset Postmodernism boldly announced the end of the Modern tradition. It was a new quest for significance, meaning and belonging. Now some people think it is a philosophy that has passed its "sell-by" date. But this is what happens ~ the radical fringe becomes the dominant view. The profound concept becomes a matter

3

of shadows. Also, that is exactly how Postmodernism ended up. It is not that it has disappeared rather it has become mainstream and has been integrated into all aspects of life, including the Christian church. The art and literature which was bewilderingly impermanent, idiosyncratic, devious and questioning has become absorbed into mainstream culture. It is no longer conspicuous but is nevertheless present.

Those who suggest that Postmodernism is dead and crying out for a decent burial are naïve. Courses in Postmodernism are featured in the prospectuses of many western universities. Until recently, I taught a course entitled "Preaching Christ in a Postmodern Culture" ~ a course which I designed, based on my book of the same title.[2]

At secular universities, such courses include postmodern fiction in English departments. But postmodernism also features in sociology and philosophy departments. However when one looks more closely, one finds that many of these English literature courses, for example, are comparative in as much as they are designed to explore the relationship between postmodern and contemporary fiction. This indicates that postmodern fiction is a particular genre that relates to a particular period in the past.

Perhaps Postmodernism has lost some of its creative impetus, but its effects are permanent. It is not that Postmodernism is no longer relevant, rather it is a building block in an ongoing super-structure of thought. As such, it is something that is built upon rather than discarded. Many people still believe in postmodern ideas. Many academics will not relinquish their love of the eminent Postmodernist, Foucault. Some say there is a compelling case to be made that Postmodernism is dead by looking outside the academy at current cultural production.

---

[2] Taught at Tyndale Theological Seminary, Badhoevedorp, Netherlands.

But in the cultural marketplace novels, films and music may not claim to be Postmodern but the legacy of Postmodernism nevertheless influences many. People outside academic circles may not be talking about Derrida, Foucault, Baudrillard etc. but in reality they are influenced by these seminal thinkers in profound ways.

The twentieth-century was a century of change, and the pace of that change has accelerated in the twenty-first century. Technology, politics, travel, globalization, the media, and many other forces continue to change the world in which we live. Whether we get on a plane and fly to distant places, stay home and watch T.V., have dinner in an ethnic restaurant, or surf the internet, we encounter different cultures every day. Whatever we do, we are continually reminded that our view of the world is but one of many perspectives.

With the emergence of multicultural societies comes interaction with different belief-systems and religions. Values like mutual respect, tolerance and a dislike of dogmatism have become key operating concepts in society.

Underlying all these changes is a change in worldview, and this change is affecting every area of life. It changes the way we think and the way we process information. It influences the way we believe and what we believe. It alters the way we make decisions and the way we set our values and priorities. The world is transitioning from the Modern era to the Postmodern era. Such changes only occur every few hundred years or so, and when they do, they have far-reaching effects. It fundamentally alters the socio-political, religious and psychological landscapes.

Definition of Modernism

Modernity was the philosophical framework marked by rationalism, scientific research, technological advancement and economic progress. Modernism was also the era in which evangelicalism as a movement came into being, grew up, and matured into what it is today.[3] Evangelicals made it their concern to reach people with the gospel, understanding the mandate to "make disciples of all nations" (Mt. 28:19). In doing so, they wrestled with the Modern context in which they lived. In the course of the years, evangelicals devised strategies and organizational structures that they felt were adequate for the task.

Definition of Postmodernism

In the last decades of the twentieth-century, however, Modernism gave way to a new era and philosophy, called Postmodernism. As a philosophy, Postmodernism is strongly reactionary against Modernism. The search for objective truth is replaced with the celebration of subjective truth. As an era, Postmodernism is defined by the desire to create a society in which peoples of all cultures, races and belief systems can coexist peacefully.

So what?

Many evangelicals today are aware of this new Postmodern context, which is increasingly replacing Modernism. Having been conditioned to interact with Modernism for centuries by an exhaustive body of literature, and self-perpetuating organizational structures, many evangelicals have realized that something has fundamentally changed. We are confronted with radical changes in education, art, and entertainment. The result is that many Christians are confused and experiencing a sense of alienation from the world as they knew it.

---

[3] There are many writers that support this idea: see e.g. Dave Tomlinson, *The Post Evangelical* (London, England: Triangle, 1995), 72; Stanley J. Grenz, 161; Alistair McGrath, *A Passion for Truth - The Intellectual Coherence of Evangelicalism*, (Downer's Grove, Illinois: Intervarsity Press, 1996), 166-73.

Evangelicals understand that their witness needs to be credible and understandable to the people they are trying to reach. They had successfully contextualized the gospel for the Modern world and now face a new challenge, to contextualize it for the postmodern era. While Postmodernism has been changing the way people think, many evangelicals still try to reach persons with a Modernist approach to the world. This has caused a cultural breakdown in communication resulting in the increasing marginalization of evangelicals in society. Thus, the message of the gospel appears to be irrelevant, and it is consequently ignored.

Evangelicals need to understand how the world around them has changed. If we are to reach the people of our world with the gospel, we must understand that they no longer have a Modern worldview, but a Postmodern one, and we must understand what that worldview is. If we fail to do so, our message will simply be unintelligible to our audience.

Understanding Contemporary Culture

To reach Postmodern people, Christians need to understand their context once again, and need to know how to communicate effectively to Postmodern people. We need to understand Modernism and Postmodernism, to see how they are distinguished, and to explore how the gospel needs to be contextualized for the Postmodern era. The central question is: "What is Postmodernism, and how can Christians reach Postmodern people in the Postmodern world?"

The Purpose of This Book

The purpose of this book is to help Christians understand the Postmodern worldview and find ways to reach Postmodern people. With this in mind, we need to understand the Modern and Postmodern worldviews and how they are distinguished. Furthermore, we need to understand reasons why the Modern worldview is being exchanged for the Postmodern worldview. With an understanding of the Postmodern worldview, one can then seek to understand Postmodern people and the types of communication and community to which they might be receptive. Believers need to approach the twenty-first century with the same attitude that the apostle Paul had in the first century:

1 Corinthians 9:19-23

[19] For though I am free from all men, I have made myself a slave to all, so that I may gain more. [20] And so to the Jews I became as a Jew, that I might gain Jews; to those under the law I became as under the law, though I myself am not under the law, that I might gain those under the law. [21] To those without law I became as without law, although I am not without law toward God but under the law toward Christ, that I might gain those without law. [22] To the weak I became weak, that I might gain the weak. I have become all things to all men, that I might by all means save some. [23] But I do all things for the sake of the gospel, that I may become a fellow partaker of it.

Limitations

We will interact with a broad spectrum of opinions and approaches to the subject, but that interaction will not be exhaustive. This work is an introduction to the subject but for those who wish to read more a short bibliography is provided. While an in-depth study of Postmodernism as a philosophy, or the way in which Postmodernism influences society, would be fascinating, discussion of these will be limited to what is relevant to the central question of this book.[4] The same goes for some of the tensions that the Postmodern worldview has with the Christian worldview. It would be very interesting to discuss all the implications of Postmodern thinking in relation to what Christians believe, but we will limit the discussion to what is important with regards to evangelism.

---

[4] For an in-depth study of how Postmodernism influences all aspects of society, see Dennis McCallum, ed., *The Death of Truth* (Minneapolis, Minnesota: Bethany House Publishers, 1996).

CHAPTER 1 Modernism

From Modernism to Postmodernism

"The times, they are a-changing", sang Bob Dylan in 1964. It was the time of the hippies, of free love and flower-power. It was also the time of the Vietnam War, the Cold War, and of questioning authority. It was a time when nuclear arsenals were threatening the very existence of the world. Air travel brought us into contact with diverse cultures and television brought the world into our homes. And while scientific research had advanced to the point of putting a man on the moon, the West became increasingly aware of major world problems such as starvation and dictatorial regimes in places around the world.

Less obvious, but more profound, was the change that was taking place in the background. While many celebrated this marvelous and incredible achievement, there was also an increasing disquiet that Modernism did not deliver the expected utopia. There had been two world wars, a Holocaust, the development of nuclear power and a cold war. Confronted with this less than wonderful heritage of Modernism many people sought and found a different road in the writings of philosophers like Jacques Derrida and Francois Lyotard, and a different worldview was gradually emerging. This paradigm became known as Postmodernism, and it started to replace the old paradigm of Modernism. First taught in universities, it soon became a significant influence on many academic studies, affecting professors and students together, and thus trickling out into society. There it subtly but profoundly started impacting culture, belief systems, decision-making processes, government, art, religion, entertainment, business, information management, scientific research, moral standards, relationships, and many other areas of public and private life. "Modernism," says Gene Edward Veith, "is being replaced by the new secular ideology of Postmodernism. This new set of assumptions ...

is gaining dominance throughout our culture."[5] Thus, an old era gave way to a new, the era of Postmodernism. Bob Dylan's prophetic voice (along with the voices and music of many others) championed a protest movement in song. Indeed the times were changing.[6]

What makes this transition so difficult to observe and to describe is that Postmodernism is both a critique of, and a continuation from the Modern era. It is not a violent revolution that establishes Postmodernism in the place of Modernism. Rather, it is a very gradual moving away from the principles of Modernism and adopting new principles; ones that are part of what the world is rapidly getting to know as Postmodernism. As Thomas observed:

> In Postmodern orthodoxy, we take for granted the achievements of Modernity, of Modern methods of inquiry, Modern procedures of searching scientifically for truth, and Modern assumptions about a just democratic political order.[7]

The transition to Postmodernism is both a rejection of Modernism, and a search for an alternative way of thinking, living and seeing the world. Postmodernism is not "a moving away" from Modernism, but rather "a moving beyond." As Thomas Oden continues:

> The axiom of Postmodern consciousness is not that Modernity is corrupt, but that it is defunct, obsolete, passé, antiquated ... It is not merely a

---

[5] Gene Edward Veith, Jr., *Postmodern Times - A Christian Guide to Contemporary Thought and Culture* (Wheaton, Illinois: Crossway Books, 1994), 19.

[6] Walter Truett Anderson, *Reality Isn't What It Used To Be*, (New York: Harper Collins Publishers, 1992), 44.

[7] Thomas Oden, "The Death of Modernity and Postmodern Evangelical Spirituality," in *The Challenge of Postmodernism - An Evangelical Engagement*, ed., David S. Dockery (Wheaton, Illinois: BridgePoint, 1995), 20.

censorious, embittered, negative emotional reaction against Modernity. That would mistake the Postmodern orthodox premise entirely. Note carefully: there is no reason to be opposed to something that is already dead.[8]

Worldviews and Miscommunication

If we are to reach people in the Postmodern era with the gospel, it is important that we understand they no longer hold to a Modern philosophical framework or pursue the Modern dream. The Postmodern world is increasingly becoming the new environment in which people live, and such an environment has a conditioning effect. People are both influenced by their context, and participate in the process that proliferates and develops it. If indeed Modernism and Postmodernism both are worldviews that condition the way people live, the way they think, the way they process information, the way they arrive at conclusions and the way they make decisions, then an understanding of each will greatly benefit those who are actively involved in the disciple-making process. As David Hesselgrave states: "Our worldview, then, is the way we see ourselves in relation to all else. Conversely, it is the way we see all else in relation to ourselves."[9]

Both Modernism and Postmodernism are worldviews, and both are very powerful in their own way. Some writers have complained that evangelicals are relatively ignorant of the transition that is taking place, and that they still use tools and strategies that were devised to reach Modern people while the people they are attempting to reach are in

---

[8] Ibid.

[9] David J. Hesselgrave, *Communicating Christ Cross-Culturally - an Introduction to Missionary Communication*, 2d ed. (Grand Rapids, Michigan: Zondervan, 1991), 199.

the process of, or have already migrated to a different worldview:

> Evangelicalism has been affected in much the same way by the Enlightenment. Certain central Enlightenment ideas appear to have been uncritically taken on board by some evangelicals, with the result that part of the movement runs the risk of becoming a secret prisoner of a secular outlook which is now dying before our eyes.[10]

The results are obvious: not only is there miscommunication, but Christians are effectively marginalizing themselves, making their message appear out of touch and obsolete in the eyes of the world.

This need not be so, or, if we allow for the fact that the message itself is opposed to this world and its rulers, it need not be so to the extent that it is.[11] An understanding of what Modernism and Postmodernism are, and what the implications of the transitions from the former to the latter are, will set the stage for a discussion of means, methods and strategies Christians deploy to reach those who live around them.

The Modern Era

Postmodernism follows the era that in Western thought and culture has become known as Modernism. Finding proper dates for Modernism is an interesting effort, as different authors give different dates. Part of the confusion stems from the fact that the transition from one era to the next is never a black-and-white distinction, but rather a process. The confusion over Modernism's dates is also a result of disagreement over definition: do we consider the

---

[10] Alistair McGrath, *A Passion for Truth - The Intellectual Coherence of Evangelicalism*. (Downer's Grove, Illinois: Intervarsity Press, 1996), 173.

[11] John 12:31.

Enlightenment as part of Modernism? Could we consider the Renaissance part of the Modern era? As an era Modernism, defined in its widest sense, stands as the transition between the Middle- Ages and the current period. Modernism can be seen as an attempt to reconstruct the world in the perceived absence of God. This absence can be seen in some of the historical developments for which Modernism is remembered as scientific research starts to lay bare the secrets of the cosmos. Humanism teaches the value of man apart from his divine image. Evolutionary thinking discovers the origin of man, once more negating any human need for God. Technological advance culminates in the destruction of Hiroshima and Nagasaki on the one side, and the walking of a man on the moon on the other.

Oden dates Modernism from the storming of the Bastille to the fall of the Berlin wall.

> The duration of the epoch of Modernity is now clearly identifiable as a precise two-hundred-year period between 1789 and 1989, between the French revolution and the collapse of communism. Such dating is always disputable… but this one cries out with clarity. The analogies between the revolutions of 1789 and 1989 will intrigue historians for centuries to come.[12]

In placing such clear dates on Modernism Oden takes a very specific view of the end of Modernism. Others, like Grenz and Veith, recognize that we are currently in a transition from the Modern era to the Postmodern era. If

---

[12] Thomas Oden, *Between two World - Notes on the death of Modernity in America and Russia* (Downer's Grove, Illinois: InterVarsity Press, 1992), 32.

we are indeed in transition, then Modernism still plays a role in today's society, albeit a receding one.[13]

Key Aspects of Modernism

The following characteristics identify modernism:

Rationalism

Rationalism, with its emphasis on human intellectual ability meant that the mind became the arbiter of truth, and replaced the need for Scripture as source of authority. This way of thinking started with Renee Descartes (1596-1650), who, in his effort to reduce reality to a set of mathematical principles, coined his famous dictum, "cogito, ergo sum" ("I think, therefore I am"). While Descartes himself was a Christian, his philosophical deliberations exalted the human being to a position of supremacy, making him autonomous, and relegating God to the fringes of reality.[14] In so doing, rationalism became the foundation of that period in Western thought called the Enlightenment. Characterized by reason, scientific discovery and human autonomy, the Enlightenment embraced classical thinking with its order and rationality, while at the same time lumping Christianity with paganism as outdated superstition. Reason, it was

---

[13] It is however interesting to discuss the extent to which this transition is nearing its completion. Answers to that probably depend on where one is in the world. One could argue that in much of Western Europe (most notably France, The Netherlands and the United Kingdom, Australia and New Zealand), as well as some of the bigger cities in the U.S. (New York, Chicago, Los Angeles) the transition from Modernism to Postmodernism as the main cultural driving force is now working towards completion.

[14] See Stanley J. Grenz Grenz, *Primer on Postmodernism* (Grand Rapids, Michigan: Eerdrnans, 1996), 63; D.A Carson, *The Gagging of God* (Grand Rapids, Michigan: Zondervan, 1996), 63-66, 58-60.

thought, would liberate mankind out of reliance on the supernatural.[15]

Humanism

The emphasis on human autonomy was only the start of a whole new view of human beings that was distinctly different from biblical teaching. An emphasis on the essential goodness of mankind replaced the view of moral depravity. This basic human goodness would cause man to make good and healthy choices, contributing to progress and the eradication of evil. An important part of humanism was a shift in attention from the corporate structure to the individual. "Autonomous individualism", says Oden, "focuses on the detached individual as a self-sufficient, sovereign self."[16] With God out of the picture, there was no longer any need for the individual to live for a goal outside of himself. Instead, there is now no higher goal than personal happiness. Modernism, says Oden, was characterized by a constant search for pleasure of the self.[17]

Reductive Naturalism

With God out of the way, and a fundamental belief in the explicability of everything through human research, Modern man viewed reality as a clock; "we may not know how it works yet, but we'll find out." The universe became a matter of cause and effect. Reductive Naturalism, says Oden, is that view that reduces all forms of knowing to laboratory experiments, empirical observation or quantitative analysis. It is the reduction of sex to orgasm,

---

[15] Gene Edward Veith, Jr., 33.

[16] Thomas Oden, 33.

[17] Op. Cit., 34.

persons to bodies, psychology to stimuli, economics to planning mechanics, and politics to machinery.[18]

Absolute Moral Relativism

One thing has to lead to another, and, as Oden concludes, the logical outcome of all this is absolute moral relativism. If there is no God creating and ordering reality, then man is left to his own devices. Such relativism, says Oden, views all morals as merely relative to the changing, processing determinants of human cultures. It is dogmatically absolute in its moral relativism because it asserts that relativism uncritically.[19]

Scientific Research and Technological Advancement

Faith in human supremacy led to a desire to master that universe. Newtonian physics ushered in a clockwork view of reality, opening everything from outer-space to the inner parts of physical and psychological man to the eye of the empirical researcher.

Belief in Progress

There was a reason for the zeal with which Modern man applied himself to science, namely the belief that ultimately science would lead to the eradication of hunger, war, poverty, inequality, oppression, and every other evil in this world. Such Positivism was evident in John F. Kennedy's inaugural address when he declared: "The world

---

[18] Op. Cit., 35.

[19] Ibid.

is very different now. For man holds the power to abolish all forms of human poverty."[20]

With science as its guide, mankind would come to its full potential. Science, writes Stanley Grenz, coupled with the power of education, would eventually free us from our vulnerability to nature, as well as from all social bondage.[21] The effort to come to the point in history where such evils would no longer exist was termed "the Enlightenment project".[22]

Superiority over other cultures

Scientific research brought means to travel far and this in turn brought us into contact with other cultures. Modern man viewed those cultures with a sense of superiority. On the one side there was the mission to bring progress to places that had not tasted it which made it morally correct for Modern man to conquer territories far away, taking whatever resources were needed and reducing those of other cultures and convictions to laborers.

National Organizations

An important aspect of Modernism often missed, is that it was Modern thought that was inspirational in the emergence of nation-states as a product of the Modern era. The Modern era, writes Strphen Toulmin, began with the

---

[20] Michael Sandel, "America's Search for a New Public Philosophy" *Atlantic Monthly*, March 1996, 66. Quoted in Jimmy Long, *Generating Hope - A Strategy for Reaching the Postmodern Generation* (Downer's Grove, Illinois: InterVarsity Press, 1997), 64.

[21] Grenz, 4. In a very insightful look at one of Holywood's more popular television series, Grenz makes a link between Star Trek and Modernism. "Like Modern fiction in general, the original Star Trek series reflected many aspects of the Enlightenment project and of late Modernity. The crew of the Enterprise included persons of various nationalities working together for the common benefit of humankind, (*A Primer on Postmodernism*), 5.

[22] Grenz, 58.

creation of separate, independent sovereign states, each of them organized around a particular nation, with its own language and culture, maintaining a government that was legitimated as expressing the national will, or national traditions or interests.[23]

Modernism from a Christian Point of View

Postmodernism issues a verdict on Modernism in every way: Modernism did not deliver what it promised. In many ways then Postmodernism is a critique of Modernism and a turning to a different path.

Living on the edge between the Modern and the Postmodern worlds, we have a unique opportunity. Times of transition make people insecure and during such times of insecurity we can sometimes see some of the motivations that drive people to do what they are doing. As Christians, our worldview is neither Modern nor Postmodern and so we have an ability to look in from the outside. What we see is, people looking for the means to bring about that world in which everyone will have enough, there will be no more war and injustice, and happiness will be accessible to all. From a Christian point of view, it can seem as if people are looking for paradise, but a paradise without God. To adopt a biblical image, it is as if we want to go back to the Garden of Eden, but without ceasing our rebellion. Because it is impossible to return to paradise without making peace with God, such efforts are in fact futile. There is no redemption without God. Modernism, therefore, to the extent that it was an attempt to bring about paradise, was doomed from the start.

---

[23] Stephen Toulmin, *Cosmopolis*.Chicago, Illinois: Inversity of Chicago Press, 1990, 7. For a very similar list see Millard J. Erickson, *PostModernizing the Faith: Evangelical Responses to the Challenge of Postmodernism* (Grand Rapids, Michigan: Baker Books, 1998), 16-17.

In making man the center of the universe, it would seem that Modernism was actually very much a continuation of our rebellion against God. From a biblical perspective, we can say that Modernism was another expression of the fall. In exalting the supremacy and autonomy of mankind, declaring human independence from God, Modernism is nothing short of another affirmation of our choice to eat the fruit of the tree of the knowledge of Good and Evil in the Genesis 3 account. Modernism will not lead us to heaven, and there is no utopia just around the corner - in essence, Modernism is just another stage in man's rebellion against God.

Three writers, seeking to develop a biblical view of Modernism and Postmodernism, see Modernism as a new tower of Babel ~ an attempt to build a city without God.[24] Just as the story of Babel (recounted in Genesis 11:1-9) summarizes the primordial cultural aspirations of the human race in terms of the building of "a city with a tower reaching to the heavens", so we could characterize the Modern Western dream of progress as the building of a vast, towering civilization, a social and cultural accomplishment of immense, even mythic proportions.[25]

---

[24] Gene Edward Veith, Jr., 20; Richard J. Middleton and Brian J. Walsh, *Truth is Stranger Than It Used to Be* (Downers Grove, Illinois: Intervarsity Press, 1995), 15.

[25] Middleton and Walsh, 15.

CHAPTER 2 Transition ~ The Nature of the Chances

Walter Truett Anderson has said, "We are in the midst of a great, confusing, stressful and enormously promising historical transition."[26] While all around us the world is changing as a result of technological advances, political developments and globalization, a change in worldviews is also taking place in the world around us. Perhaps less obvious, but all the more influential and profound, this change is taking place in the way people think, the way we do scientific research, the way we organize our societies politically and socio-economically, the way we believe and profess what we believe, the way we advertise, the way we relate to those of other cultures or other persuasions, and in many more ways. "People rarely understand or even notice great historical transitions as they are taking place", writes Anderson: "it is said that Louis XVI, at the end of the day the Bastille fell, wrote in his diary: 'Rien' (nothing happened)."[27]

However, much is happening, and the developments are of great importance to those who would seek to reach others with the gospel of Jesus Christ, in their effort to disciple all nations.[28] All over the world, people are now discovering that strategies that have worked for decades do so no longer. Stanley Grenz says:

> Many social observers agree that the West is in the midst of change. In fact, we are apparently

---

[26] Walter Truett Anderson, *The Truth about the Truth*, (New York: Tacher Putnam Books, 1995), 2.

[27] Ibid.

[28] The need to make disciples of all nations as commanded by Jesus in the Great Commission as found in Matthew 28:18-20 is the fundamental starting point. Understanding those we seek to reach is logically the first step in the disciple-making effort.

experiencing a cultural shift that rivals the innovations that marked the birth of Modernity out of the decay of the Middle Ages: we are in the midst of the transition of the Modern to the Postmodern era.[29]

As Diogenes Allen has observed:

A massive intellectual revolution is taking place that is perhaps as great as that which marked the Modern world from the Middle Ages. The foundations of the Modern world are collapsing, and we are entering a Postmodern world. The principles forged during the Enlightenment (c.1600 1780), which formed the foundation of the Modern mentality, are crumbling.[30]

Unfortunately, laments Dennis McCallum, Christians are oblivious to these changes. He compares it to the effect the publication of Charles Darwin *Origin of the Species* had on the world. While the theory of evolution transformed the world, it took Christians a long time to perceive what was happening all around them.

...within months [of publication of 'Origins of the Species'] the scientific world was going through a revolution in thinking. Although at the time, most Christians had no idea anything was happening, no one doubts today the far-reaching results of that revolution. During the next few decades after Darwin, the notion of naturalistic evolution became a new consensus among intellectuals, eventually affecting every academic discipline, education, government and even the church...

---

[29] Stanley J. Grenz, *A Primer on Postmodernism* (Grand Rapids, Michigan: Eerdmans Publishing Company, 1995), 2.

[30] Diogenes Allen, *Christian Belief in a Postmodern World - The Full Wealth of Conviction* (Louisville, Westminster: John Knox Press, 1989) 2.

Now, in the late twentieth century, we face a new revolution that likely will dwarf Darwinism in its impact on every aspect of thought and culture ... Once again, Christians are not ready for a major challenge to the Christian worldview.[31]

What Grenz, Allen, and McCallum have in common is the awareness that the transition from Modernism to Postmodernism is phenomenal in its effects and implications. It is almost impossible to overestimate the way Postmodernism will change the world in which we live. Many Christians have observed these changes and have expressed their concern over them. Unfortunately, there appears to be no way back.[32] Walter Truett Anderson writes:

The conservative indictment is correct, and yet the strategy that follows from it - to rebuild consensus, to get a core of standard values and beliefs in place in every American mind - is doomed to fail ... Humpty-Dumpty is not going to be put back together again.[33]

We cannot stop the world from moving on. The Modern age was not such a great one! Should we not rather develop an understanding of what Postmodernism is,

---

[31] Dennis McCallum, *The Death of Truth: What's Wrong With Multiculturalism, the Rejection of Reason and the New Postmodern Diversity* (Minneapolis, Minnesota: Bethany House Publishers, 1996). This quote was on the web at http://www.crossrds.org/chl.htm on 28 November 1997.

[32] Many conservatives are now becoming convinced of this as well. In an open letter dated February 16, 1999, to hundreds of conservative Christians in the U.S, Paul Weyrich, head of the Free Congress Foundation, writes: "We have lost the culture wars." He then considers various options, and recommends that Christians seek ways to withdraw from society. Weyrich recommended the name `Moral Majority' for the movement headed by Jerry Falwell. In his letter he states: "There is no moral majority." For more information, see http://www.freedixie.net/weyrich.html.

[33] Walter Truett Anderson, *Reality Isn't What It Used To Be* (New York: Harper Collins Publishers, 1992), 4-5.

learn the ways in which it is hostile to Christianity, discover the new inroads it will offer to the gospel, and find the ways in which we can be effective witnesses to Postmodern people?

What is interesting about this transition is that evangelicals demonstrate a definite sense of uneasiness when they are confronted with these or other expressions of Postmodernism. Could it be that evangelicals are stuck in a "time-warp", as Tomlinson suggests, still desperately trying to be relevant to a world that has ceased to exist?[34]

One thing is for sure, as Dave Tomlinson states, "Those who think that Postmodernism is a figment of the academic imagination, a passing intellectual fad, could not be more wrong. Postmodernism has flowed right out of the musty corridors of academia into the world of popular culture."[35]

What Brought the Changes About?

Evangelical Christians typically think they have very little in common with Postmodernists. They cannot understand the Postmodern belief that truth is relative, and they have a distaste for the desire of Postmodern politicians to create a society in which every lifestyle is accepted, while none is dominant (cultural pluralism). Most evangelical authors writing on the subject of Postmodernism argue that it is important to maintain the coherent and absolute nature of truth, and in doing so basically reject the whole Postmodern worldview.

This is understandable, but a simplistic dismissal of Postmodernism demonstrates a lack of understanding of the issues that people are facing, and it ignores the necessity to explore new ways of living together and moving forward.

---

[34] Dave Tomlinson, *The Post-Evangelical* (London, United Kingdom: Triangle, 1995), 79.

[35] Op. Cit., 75.

We must understand that the Modern worldview is simply not an option anymore.

If we are to reach people with a Postmodern mindset, we must understand the way they think. We have to understand the historical and sociological necessity that drove them to accept a Postmodern worldview in the first place.

Science

Perhaps it is surprising that it was the chief of the Modern endeavors, science itself, which started challenging the Modernist worldview. In 1900, Max Planck published a series of scientific explanations that would become the basis for Einstein's relativity theory, which would give birth to the study of Quantum Mechanics. The acceptance of Quantum Mechanics theory into mainstream science necessitated a reconsideration of Newtonian physics. The latter had been the logical companion and product of the Modernist worldview and had actually served as the foundation for a great many inventions and discoveries. But Quantum Mechanics questioned the simplicity and unitary nature of physics, arguing instead for the complexity and multiplicity of physics. While we are not conducting a thorough investigation of the many ways in which Quantum Mechanics challenged the Western Modern mindset, a simple example will be helpful. Max Planck's hypothesis was that atoms emit and absorb energy only in discrete bundles (quanta) instead of continuously, as was held by classical physics. Quantum theory thus proposes a dual nature for both waves and particles, with one aspect predominating in some situations and the other predominating in other situations. This concept was unheard of under the regime of Newtonian physics and caused quite a paradigm shift in scientific circles. Quantum theory was born, and our view of the world has not been the same since.[36]

In an, even more, amazing move, Einstein then took Planck's conclusions and used them as the foundation of his own thinking. Based on Planck's work Einstein formulated his famous $E=mc^2$. That simple formula shook the scientific world more than anything hitherto did, as it basically proposed the interchangeable nature of matter and energy; something that was impossible under the regime of Newtonian physics. Anderson writes:

> Einstein's challenge to common-sense reality was far greater than Galileo's: he asked us to believe that time and space were not all that we ordinarily experienced them to be, that matter and energy were the same, and up and down merely relative notions.[37]

Another paradigm shift was caused by the formulation of the Uncertainty Principle by Werner Heisenberg. Originally formulated solely for the field of Quantum Mechanics, the principle was soon introduced to many other fields of scientific research where it had a profound impact. Stated simply, this principle holds that it is impossible to make an accurate statement about the location of a particle and the momentum of that particle at the same time. The effect of this principle is to convert the laws of physics into statements about relative principles instead of absolute certainties.

As this principle worked its way through the academic community, it came to mean that no researcher was able to investigate a subject without impacting that subject in one way or another. While this did not make scientific research irrelevant, it proved to be a paradigm shift, particularly for

---

[36] Grenz, 51.

[37] Anderson, 36.

those involved in the humanities. Nowhere else is it as easy to see that a researcher often impacts a research subject by investigating it, thus influencing, and frequently distorting, his results. A psychologist influences a participant in a research project by asking him questions and taking him or her out of her normal environment. The mere presence of an anthropologist in a tribe has already affected the very life of the tribe he is trying to study. How can a researcher, whose presence and actions have impacted the research subject, however subtly, make any absolute statements about his findings? And can we trust the results of scientific research as true? This perception caused many to look at science with a quizzical eye and ask the question: "Is there such a thing as pure scientific knowledge?"

This question was asked in an atmosphere in which people were shocked with the destructive abilities of science. The atomic bombing of Hiroshima and Nagasaki caused many to reexamine their view of science as good and progressive. In the Modern dream, it was the object of science to help bring about a better world for all. But instead, under the excellent leadership of Oppenheimer who brought together the best physicists from all over the world, such enormously destructive powers were developed that human life was threatened on a grand scale. The ensuing Cold War did little to re-establish trust in science: as time progressed the public was bombarded with facts that told us of how many times each side was able to destroy the entire planet. Was this evolution? Was Life evolving to ever higher forms of life, to where it finally was able to exterminate all life? Trust in science as the agent of hope gradually eroded. The intellectual climate changed to the point where people developed a distrust of science: science did not bring the happiness and fulfillment desired.

Worse, as the colonial empires crumbled around the world, and television brought far-away places directly into our living rooms, it became clear that time and again science served as an agent of oppression. The population of

27

the Bikini-islands suffered in numerous ways from nuclear testing in the Pacific Ocean. Jews were helpless victims of Nazi doctors desiring to understand genetics and hoping to develop the ultimate *untermensch.*[38] In many laboratories of the cosmetic industry around the world thousands of animals are the helpless victims of cruel and painful testing every day by vivisectionists, in many cases for no other reason than to develop yet another shampoo or make-up product. As the public awareness of this grew, it became clearer and clearer that science would not bring the desired utopia, and that in the wrong hands science would produce destructive results of enormous scale. Science itself came to be regarded as a violent act. In a front page article on Postmodernism, the *Wall Street Journal* quoted one Postmodern historian as saying that male science has assaulted nature like a violent man exploits a helpless woman. "A passive nature had to be interrogated, unclothed, penetrated, and compelled by man to reveal her secrets."[39]

The last reason that people started losing confidence in science was its innate inability to provide meaningful answers to the more existential questions of life.

> Science that tries to contain the whole world of truth has produced great material progress, Newbigin notes, yet it offers no idea whatsoever what it is for. Such science leaves people rich and powerful, but purposeless. In the end, this project must destroy even science.[40]

---

[38] A German word for a person considered racially or socially inferior.

[39] Dennis McCallum, "Are We Ready?" Article found on the Internet at http://www.crossrds.orgichl.html

[40] Tim Stafford, "God's Missionary to Us," *Christianity Today*, 40 (December 9, 1996), 24.

Historical Events

Both World Wars were historical events that led to the erosion of trust in Modernism. World War I may have been a temporary setback on the Modern agenda, but World War II made clear that the Modern agenda was doomed. "The trauma of the Holocaust is now generally seen as a powerful and shocking indictment of the pretensions and delusions of Modernity."[41]

A powerful example of such an indictment is the *Diary of Anne Frank*, which was particularly damaging to the Modern view of Man. Modernism had spawned Humanism, which held that man basically was a good being. Anne Frank, she expressed a basic enlightenment view of the nature of man when she wrote:

> It is really a wonder that I have not dropped all my ideals, because they seem so absurd and impossible to carry out. Yet I keep them, because in spite of everything I still believe that people are really good at heart. I simply can't build my hopes on a foundation consisting of confusion, misery, and death. I see the world gradually being turned into a wilderness, I hear the ever-approaching thunder, which will destroy us too, I can feel the sufferings of millions and yet, if I look up into the heavens, I think that it will all come right, that this cruelty too will end, and that peace and tranquility will return again.[42]

While Anne Frank's idealism is touching, her diary confronts us with the horror of the Holocaust. Most of us cannot understand the reasoning behind the desire to

---

[41] Alistair McGrath, *A Passion for Truth - The Intellectual Coherence of Evangelicalism*, (Downers Grove, Illinois: Intervarsity Press, 1996), 180.

[42] Anne Frank, *Anne Frank - The Diary of a Young Girl*, transl. B.M. Mooyaart-Doubleday (New York: Doubleday & Company, inc., 1967), 287.

destroy such a small girl. In the light of such atrocities, how can people living after World War II still believe in the basic goodness of man, and the basic goodness of knowledge?

Technological progress brought air travel, television, and the internet. While we celebrate our ability to travel far, see so much and be so well-informed, these things continually confront us with many different lifestyles. How different from a hundred years ago, when it was possible for a man to never meet another lifestyle in his entire life! Now we live in cities where many languages are spoken and many people-groups and nationalities are represented. Moreover, even those of our own culture, language and skin color have grouped themselves and are divided by lines of wealth, age, sexual preference, political conviction, religious affiliation, etc.

We are confronted with war, poverty, refugees, homelessness, etc. through the media on a regular basis. This demonstrates that we have nowhere near achieved the utopia of the Modern dream. Four-fifths of the world lives below the poverty-line.[43] The Modern period was also a period of exploitation through colonization, and many feel the exploitation continues to this day. The rice farmer in Indonesia and the coffee plantation worker in South America carry the same burden: to survive on wages not enough to sustain a family. Both resort to having more children, in the hope that their children will take care of them in their old age. This dynamic causes the third-world population to explode, and the people in the West regard this explosion with some degree of fear. How can we all live together on such a small planet, when there are not enough resources?

---

[43] For more information, see "Indicators on income and economic activity", a United Nations website, at http://www.un.org/Depts/unsdisocial/inc-eco.htm. Also visit the World Health Organization website at www.who.ch and the UNESCO website at www.unesco.org

Anthropology

"If any single occupational group deserves the credit - or the blame - for bringing us into the Postmodern era", writes Walter Truett Anderson, "it is the anthropologists. They created a new profession out of the study of otherness, and their findings have made it impossible for any literate person to believe there is only one way of seeing the world."[44]

As the Colonial period came to an end, people in the West looked upon those not living in the West with a new interest. The sense of superiority crumbled as the awareness grew that it wasn't getting better for everyone in the world, but just for a select minority. As new countries and people, groups made their presence known and demanded their autonomy, interest in the phenomenon of culture soared. Anderson Observed:

> The early anthropologists were the true pioneers of the twentieth century, going out in search of culture shock, exposing themselves to it in the same valiant careless way a scientist might expose himself to disease. They invented "participant observation", a brilliant addition to the human mind's repertoire of ways to making itself uncomfortable.[45]

The result for those who pondered what anthropology discovered, says Anderson, was deep psychological disturbance. They saw overwhelming evidence that different people had constructed entirely different systems of value and belief, knowledge, and myth. Inevitably, those who absorbed this material revised not only their ideas

---

[44] Anderson, 53.

[45] Op. Cit., 37.

about exotic peoples, but also their ideas about themselves.[46]

The confrontation with people who believed in their worldview with the same conviction that people in the West believed in the Modern worldview caused many to question the nature and power of worldviews in the first place. "We became persuaded that we all were in possession of something called a worldview - or that it was in possession of us," writes Anderson. The worldview became something to worry about, defend, change, or, in some cases, demolish.[47]

And so, anthropology gave rise to a new academic discipline, the sociology of knowledge. This discipline brought to the world the insight that anthropologists, in discovering and describing other cultures, invent their own.[48] This quickly translated into the concept of Socially Constructed Reality: the idea that reality is not so much objective and real, as that it is constructed in our minds, and that our worldview determines the way we experience the world. This concept quickly became very important in the Postmodern world; indeed, it became a cornerstone-understanding in the Postmodern worldview.

Philosophy

Philosophical events precipitated the fall of Modernism and the rise of Postmodernism. If Modernism started with Renee Descartes, Erasmus, and Newton, it ended with Nietzche, Freud, Marx and Bultmann. They not only served the world, says Thomas Oden, with criticism of Modernism,

---

[46] Ibid.

[47] Op. Cit., 44-45.

[48] Roy Wagner, "the Idea of Culture," in *The Truth about the Truth*, ed. Walter Truett Anderson (New York: Tacher Putnam Books, 1995), 57.

but their criticism also became the foundation on which Postmodern philosophers would continue.[49]

Friedrich Nietzsche (1844-1900) was the most influential of the four. Kurt Richardson calls Nietzsche the prophet of Postmodernity[50] and Grenz calls him the "patron saint of Postmodern philosophy,"[51] and says that the publication of *Thus spoke Zarathustra* spelled "the beginning of the end of Modernity, and the inauguration of the gestation period of Postmodernity."[52] Nietzche's contributions are myriad and his influence reaches far into popular culture. His view that religion is an expression of weakness while egotistic self-assertiveness is the most blessed human condition, says Oden, is the toxic heritage Nietzsche left behind.[53]

Grenz lists three themes in which Nietzsche contributed to the development of the Postmodern intellectual climate:[54]

- **The demise of the Enlightenment concept of truth.** Nietzsche was a philologist, and his study of words and language led him to a different understanding of truth than the one generally held up to that point. He rejected the Enlightenment concept of truth in denying the so-called correspondence-theory of truth (i.e. that

---

[49] Thomas Oden, *Between two World - Notes on the death of Modernity in America and Russia*, 36. Oden lists Bultmann as one of the four, I have substituted Bultmann for Sartre.

[50] Kurt A. Richardson, "Disorientation in Christian Belief: The Problem of De-Traditionalization in the Postmodern Context," in *The Challenge of Postmodernism - An Evangelical Engagement*, ed., David S. Dockery (Wheaton, Illinois: BridgePoint, 1995), 58.

[51] Grenz, 88.

[52] Op. Cit., 83.

[53] Oden, 36.

[54] The following discussion is based on Grenz, 89 ff.

what we see and observe accurately corresponds to what is really there). We make use of words to describe what we see, and words and language are incapable of conveying true and accurate meaning. Take for instance the word *leaf*. There are millions of variations from one leaf to another, and yet we use one word to refer to all of them. We can only grasp the concept leaf by overlooking such differences. Nietzsche, says Grenz, held that the concept "leaf" is thus actually a falsification of the reality of leaves. The problem is furthermore compounded by the fact that we not only construct individual concepts, but we then combine them into "a great edifice of ideas", in our effort to understand the world. This structure, says Nietzsche, is actually an illusion.[55]

• **The rejection of the Enlightenment concept of values.** Nietzsche rejected the objectivist understanding of values; the belief that values were more than just human agreements or inventions. All through history people had believed that values were not merely the product of human intellect, but that they stemmed from a divine order imposed on mankind. As the Judeo-Christian view became prominent in Europe, corresponding values became part of the culture and belief system. But as the Judeo-Christian worldview started losing to a secular mindset, Nietzsche noticed that this did not result in the emergence of a new set of values. Nietzche's proclamation of *The Death of God* shocked people into seeing that the disappearance of the belief in a moral God left a moral vacuum. The only thing remaining in this vacuum was a body of primitive instincts aimed at self-preservation and self-

---

[55] Grenz, 89.

promotion.[56] Because words and language are incapable of conveying true meaning (a sentiment later reiterated by other Postmodern philosophers such as Jacques Derrida and Richard Rorty) we have no access to the real world. All we have is ideas and concepts. In fact, says Grenz, he claims there is no "true world". Everything we see is a "perspectival appearance", the origin of which lies within ourselves.

• **The rejection of the Enlightenment philosopher.** The Enlightenment philosophers saw themselves as those who would facilitate the search for absolute truth, by creating the framework that would give every discovery its correct place, and which would correspond to reality in ever closer ways. But as Nietzsche rejects this view of truth, he redefines the role of the philosopher. A philosopher in Nietzsche's understanding is not one who discovers truth and places it in a coherent framework; rather, a philosopher is someone who creates a myth, an understanding that he then leads others into. While this myth or understanding has very little correspondence to reality and has no claim to correspondence, it nevertheless gives meaning to life and room for life to deploy itself.[57]

It should be clear from the above that Nietzsche has very little appreciation for religion, especially religion of the Judeo-Christian variety. In the *Notebooks* of 1873, Nietzsche writes: "What is truth? A mobile army of metaphors, metonyms and anthropomorphisms."[58]

---

[56] Op. Cit., 92.

[57] Op. Cit., 95-97.

[58] Friedrich Nietzsche, 'On Truth and Lie in an Extra Moral Sense', traditional translation (as above) in Walter Kaufmann, ed., *The Portable Nietzsche*,

Especially in religion, Nietzsche asserts that people use "errors" for their own advantage, self-interest or power.[59]

Nietzche views religion as a power-bid, an attempt to gain domination over the world around us, especially other people. In this Nietzsche follows Marx in believing that truth becomes "repressive" and he agrees with Feuerbach that it diminishes humanness. It propagates "vicious frauds...systems of cruelty on the strength of which the priest became and remains master".[60] Nietzsche's claim may be offensive to Christians, and certainly Thiselton deals with his criticism effectively, but it needs to be remembered that Nietzsche lived during a time when the nations of Europe sought to gain more and more control over the rest of the world. They did so through a system of colonization that almost always oppressed the natives, brought tremendous riches to Europe at the expense of the colonies and was often defended on the ground of Christian faith and duty.

Nietzsche's influence is clearly felt in Postmodern philosophy today. Jacques Derrida explicitly acknowledges his indebtedness to Nietzsche.[61] Thiselton states that "The Postmodern self follows Nietzsche and Freud in viewing claims to truth largely as devices which serve to legitimate power-interests. Disguise covers everything. Hence a culture of distrust and suspicion emerges."[62]

(New York; Viking Press. 1968) 46, cited by Anthony C. Thiselton, *Interpreting God and the Postmodern Self*, (Grand Rapids Michigan: Eerdmans, 1995), 12.

[59] Anthony C. Thiselton, *Interpreting God and the Postmodern Self*, (Grand Rapids Michigan: Eerdmans, 1995), 5.

[60] Op. Cit., 7.

[61] Jacques Derrida, *Of Grammatology*, (Eng: Baltimore: John Hopkins University Press, 1976), xxi, also quoted by Thiselton, 15.

[62] Thiselton, 12.

Karl Marx (1818-83)

While most cultural observers agree that communism, Marx's brainchild, has collapsed as a political and economic system, Marx's influence is still with us strongly in a number of ways. Marx introduced the concept of class struggle, and while the original categories of bourgeoisie and laborers have largely ceased to exist in Western societies, new categories, many on an international level, have come to the foreground. Marx has contributed to the Postmodern ethos the desire for social change. Anywhere where one party fills the role of "overlords" and another fills the role of "underdog" it is society's role to upset that balance and guarantee freedom for the underdog, creating equality between all. Most Postmodernists, writes Veith, intend their position to be liberating, freeing oppressed groups from the "one truth" proclaimed by oppressive forces.[63]

> While classical Marxism has been discredited in former Communist countries, it still appeals to Western intellectuals, partly no doubt out of sheer rebellion against their own societies. But theirs is a slightly different Marxism from that of Engels and Lenin. Classical Marxism believes that economic change, culminating in socialism, will transform the culture. The new Marxists, following the teachings of the Italian Communist Antonio Gramsci, teach that cultural change must precede socialism. Today's left wing shows little concern for the labor movement and economic theory, unlike the Marxists of the last generation. Instead, the Left emphasizes cultural change. Changing America's values is seen as the best means for ushering in the socialist utopia.[64]

---

[63] Veith, 159-60.

[64] Op. Cit, 161.

Marxism is present in the Postmodern ethos today inasmuch as the battle in culture, government and the media is to see that every underdog group of people be freed from domination, be they Gay, Native-American, or women.[65]

Sigmund Freud (1856-1939)

Sigmund Freud lived during a time when the Enlightenment worldview slowly replaced the Judeo-Christian worldview. Freud contributed to this transition by replacing the notion of sinful behavior with an understanding of psychological impulses. As Oden puts it, the view that morality and religion are expressions of neurotic sexual fixations is the bizarre heritage of Freudianism.[66]

Jean-Paul Sartre (1905-80)

One more influential voice needs to be mentioned, Jean-Paul Sartre, as one of the founders of Existentialism. As Veith writes, Existentialism became the philosophical basis for Postmodernism.[67]

Existentialism in a sense completed the Modernist journey to a worldview without God. Descartes laid the foundation for a worldview with man, not God at the center. With Darwin the need for God as the source of all disappeared. With Freud, sin was better explained as repressed sexuality or, at least, impulses from the deep human psyche. Existentialism came full circle, in that it stated there was no intrinsic meaning to life, to the universe. Whatever meaning life would have, held Existentialism, is the meaning you give it yourself. For Sartre

---

[65] Ibid.

[66] Oden, 37.

[67] Veith, 38

this was communism, for Heidegger, Nazism, and for Bultmann, Christianity.[68]

Postmodern philosophy would build further on this concept, slightly changing it to where it is no longer the individual giving meaning to life, but the community as a whole. This Postmodernist ideology is more than simple relativism, writes Veith. Whereas Modern existentialism teaches that the individual creates meaning, Postmodern existentialism teaches that meaning is created by *a social group and its language.*[69]

Processes Shaping the Transition

According to Walter Truett Anderson, three major processes are shaping the transition from the Modern to the Postmodern era.[70]

1. The Breakdown of Old Ways of Belief

While there are more beliefs around than ever before, the way people hold to those beliefs is changing.

> Revolutions of belief are...elusive, because they take place within human minds. You don't always know what's going on, even when it is your own mind that has been the scene of the upheaval. It's quite possible, for example to go from seeing science as absolute and final truth to seeing at as an ever-changing body of ideas - a big time shift, any philosopher will tell you - without feeling that anything special has happened, without losing all confidence in scientific facts: for all practical purposes the speed of light will remain 186,000 miles per second, gravity still makes water

---

[68] Ibid.

[69] Op. Cit., 48.

[70] Anderson, *Reality Isn't What It Used To Be*, 6.

39

run downhill, and ontogeny goes right on recapitulating phylogeny. It's equally possible to move from one timeless truth to seeing it as the product of a certain culture -and still happily worship at your church or temple.[71]

As we have established the idea of continual progress through rational and empirical investigation, culminating in the discovery of some form of utopia, has been shown to be false. Postmodernism is the boy crying foul in the story of the Emperor's new clothes.

Instead of one claim to truth, our societies face many truth-claims and many worldviews. There is no consensus on a single worldview, no center to rally around. Anderson, like many others, quotes Yeats', "*The Second Coming*":

Turning and turning in the widening gyre
The falcon cannot hear the falconer;
Things fall apart; the centre cannot hold;
Mere anarchy is loosed upon the world,
The blood-dimmed tide is loosed, and everywhere
The ceremony of innocence is drowned;
The best lack of all conviction, while the worst
Are full of passionate intensity.[72]

"The centre cannot hold" is the statement that best describes the Postmodern critique of Modernism. There is no center; no one place where everything comes together, and from where there can be or will be a coherent, perfect view of the Truth. The idea of objectivism, the belief that there is such a thing as entirely objective knowledge which is accessible to us - seems to be disappearing.[73] In this

---

[71] Anderson, *The Truth about the Truth*, 2.

[72] William Butler Yeats, "The Second Coming" in Richard J. Finneran, ed. *The Poems of W. B. Yeats: A New Edition* (New York: MacMillan Publishing Company, 1924), 187, as quoted by Anderson, *Reality Isn't What It Used To Be*, 6.

[73] Tomlinson, 74.

context, writes James Hunter, the "binding address of faith" has weakened. Belief has not dissolved, but the feeling of serene certainty has. Truth is no longer something unconsciously assumed, but something to which someone must consciously and intellectually assent.[74]

2. The Emergence of a New Polarization

A new conflict joins the list of race, faith, and class as causes of conflict: the conflict about the nature of truth itself. Epistemology becomes an important source of discontent: how is truth established, what is it, and how should it impact the way we live and view the world? This debate is most visible in battles over education, especially where it concerns moral instruction, says Anderson.[75]

This new polarization is clearly visible everywhere you go. It posits those who hold to "one truth, and one truth only", and who seek to have the principles of that truth govern the lives of others and society as a whole, opposite those who see many truths, and who want to create a society in which many views of truth can coexist. It can be seen in the struggle between the American Civil Liberties Union (ACLU) and Judge Moore, fundamentalist governments such as in Iran, and the government of the United States.[76] In all of these battles, says Anderson, two sides can always be determined. There are those who hold to fundamentals, the so-called Fundamentalists, and there are those who seek to construct a society in which there is room for everybody, the constructivists.[77]

---

[74] James D. Hunter, "What is Modernity? Historical roots and contemporary features", *Faith and Modernity*, eds. Philip Sampson, Vinay Samual, Chris Sugden (Oxford, United Kingdom: Regnum Books, 1994), 27.

[75] Anderson, *The Truth About The Truth*, 6.

[76] An example in Alabama a Judge insisted on hanging a plaque with the 10 commandments in his courtroom, which was protested by the ACLU.

[77] Op. Cit., 13, 268.

3. **The Birth of a Global World-Culture, with a Worldview**

Postmodernism *is* globalism, says Anderson. It is the half-discovered shape of the one unity that transcends all our differences.[78]

There is a loss of confidence in Western Culture. Newbigin is a good illustration of this. He lived long enough to witness an extraordinary loss of confidence in Western culture. When he went to India in 1936, British civilizers, heirs of the Enlightenment ruled with complete conviction that their culture – "civilization", as they referred to it - held the answers for all people. Thus, they spread education, science, law, medicine and government. Yet by the time he left India in 1974 Newbigin often saw young British "wandering in the streets as beggars dressed in unwashed Indian clothes", seeking wisdom from the East. Confidence in "civilization" had all but vanished.[79]

> The Enlightenment position retained credibility as long as people in the West assumed that theirs was the most advanced and civilized culture in the world. Moderns simply assumed that all of humankind would eventually come to appreciate and strive to attain the benefits of the Western ideal. In the Postmodern era, however, this dream is no longer credible: it has fallen prey to the phenomenon that many observers call "globalization."[80]

There are historical, scientific, sociological, philosophical and political problems that pushed men and women living at the end of the twentieth-century to

---

[78] Op. Cit., 231.

[79] Tim Stafford, "God's Missionary to Us," *Christianity Today*, 40 (December 9, 1996), 24.

[80] Grenz, 42.

abandon the Enlightenment project and search for new ways of thinking, believing, living and relating together. When one surveys the panorama of contemporary thought, it is evident in field after field, in discipline after discipline that a significant critique of Modernity has arisen along with discussion of a paradigm change.[81] The twentieth-century has been a tough time for absolutes, says Anderson: "every road that appeared to lead to certainty had some genius standing in the middle of it with a 'wrong way' sign."[82]

It is the confrontation with these problems that cause people from all walks of life to search for new answers. Postmodernism is the collective of those answers, and it is the logical outcome of that search. It is not a passing fad ~ though in time it too will pass ~ it is not merely one of many intellectual possibilities or options, although it produces all those and in some ways is defined by them.[83] For people who do not believe in the existence of a personal and loving God, but nevertheless see themselves confronted with the problems of the world the Postmodern worldview is a matter of survival, of necessity. How can one make sense of a civilization where hundreds if not thousands of different life-styles must live next to each other? Walter Truett Anderson, in his aptly named book *Reality Isn't What It Used To Be*, writes:

> Today all those cultures stand shoulder to shoulder on a single planet that now seems quite small, and another level of cultural evolution begins: it demands language about language,

---

[81] Dan R. Stiver, "The uneasy Alliance between Evangelicalism and Postmodernism: A Reply to Anthony Thiselton," in *The Challenge of Postmodernism - An Evangelical Engagement*, ed., David S. Dockery (Wheaton, Illinois: BridgePoint, 1995), 239.

[82] Anderson, *Reality*, 37.

[83] Op. Cit., 231.

religion about religions, custom about customs and a civilization to encompass civilizations.[84]

---

[84] Op. Cit., 20.

CHAPTER 3 Postmodern ~ A New Era

Why Should We Understand Postmodernism?

It is fairly difficult to describe Postmodernism without resorting to using terms to which most evangelicals have developed a severe dislike: "cultural relativism", "pluralism", and "denial of absolute truth" are but a few examples. And while some evangelicals have a good understanding of what Postmodernism actually is[85], some of those who do are actively involved in a war to try to turn the tide: away from cultural relativity, away from the moral landslide, and away from the denial of truth.[86] But most cultural experts are agreed there is no way of holding back this tide. Postmodernism is a new era in Western thought, and as such, it is here to stay for a long time. Veith divides history into three periods: the premodern (everything leading up to the Renaissance), the Modern (from the Renaissance until recently), and Postmodernism, which starts now.[87] In this view, he is far from alone. Most cultural experts, evangelical and otherwise are agreed on this division of history.[88]

---

[85]See Dennis McCallum, *The Death of Truth: What's Wrong With Multiculturalism, the Rejection of Reason and the New Postmodern Diversity* (Bethany House Publishers, 1996).

[86] Marc Driscoll. "The Flight: Characteristics of Postmodern Culture". Speech given at the 'Gen-X forum', April 29 to May 2nd, Mount Herman, California. Cassette, 1997.

[87] Gene Edward Veith, Jr., *Postmodern Times - A Christian Guide to Contemporary Thought and Culture* (Wheaton, Illinois: Crossway Books, 1994), 29-46.

[88] See for instance Oden's table of World history in Thomas Oden, *Between two Worlds - Notes on the Death of Modernity in America and Russia* (Downer's Grove, Illinois: InterVarsity Press, 1992), 51; Richard J. Middleton and Brian J. Walsh in *Truth is Stranger Than It Used to Be* (Downers Grove, Illinois: Intervarsity Press, 1995), 29; Dave Tomlinson, *The Post-Evangelical* (London, United Kingdom: Triangle, 1995), 79. Arnold Toynbee viewed the Postmodern age as the fourth and final phase of Western history and one dominated by

45

To see Postmodernism in this light, as opposed to seeing it as merely a philosophy, architectural style or political ideology helps us understand two things.[89] First of all, Postmodernism is totally pervasive in every realm of society. It's influence now reaches far beyond the French academic circles where it was born ~ it influences political discussions, academic discussions, discussion on medical ethics, discussion on philosophy of education and development, the worlds of Media and entertainment, decisions of supranational proportion, every form of artistic expression, every advertising agency and campaign, and every commitment to any ideological or religious program and faith. This is because Postmodernism is not so much the philosophy to which people are now holding, as it is the context in which all of these human activities take place.

Most importantly, Postmodernism influences every human being in the West, as well as many in the East. Not a western man, woman or child can live a life in which the influence of Postmodernism cannot be clearly seen. This is not to say that Postmodern thinking and worldview will motivate every Western individual, but it does mean that every individual will be confronted with the Postmodern culture and way of thinking, and will have to engage regularly it.

Secondly, seeing Postmodernism this way helps us understand that Christians have a new culture and philosophy to engage ~ one that will bring new challenges

---

anxiety, irrationalism and helplessness (Patricia Waugh, *Postmodernism: A Reader* (London: Edward Arnold, 1992), 5). While this is a very basic division, most authors go on to divide the Premodern and the Modern phases into various sub-phases.

[89] Strictly speaking it is actually incorrect to speak of Postmodernism as a philosophy, as there is no one discernible postmodern school of thought. Postmodernism, like Modernism, is a framework that is the product of ideas from people such as Lyotard, Derrida, Foucault, Chomsky, Rorty and others. For the sake of space and argument, though, we will speak of the postmodern worldview or philosophy.

and new opportunities. The sooner we are done resisting the inevitable ~ that is, the emergence of the Postmodern era ~ the sooner we can get on with contextualizing the gospel and finding effective ways of reaching others for Christ.

Dating Postmodernism

The term Postmodern may have first been coined in the 1930s to refer to an important historical transition already underway and as the designation for certain developments in the arts. But Postmodernism did not gain widespread attention until the 1970s. In the public consciousness, it denoted a new style of architecture. But it had invaded academic circles, originally as a label for theories expounded in University English, Philosophy and Sociology departments. Eventually, it surfaced as the description for a broader cultural phenomenon.[90]

The start of the Postmodern era is difficult to pinpoint. As we have seen before, Thomas Oden points to the fall of the Berlin Wall as the end of Modernism and the start of Postmodernism.[91] Grenz and Veith point to the demolition of the Pruitt-Igoe housing project in St. Louis, Missouri, on July 15, 1972.[92] Veith writes:

> Though a prize-winning exemplar of high technology, Modern aesthetics, and functional design, the project was so impersonal and depressing, so crime-ridden and impossible to patrol, that it was uninhabitable. The demolition of the Pruitt-Igoe development is a paradigm for Postmodernism. The Modern worldview

---

[90] Stanley J. Grenz, *Primer on Postmodernism* (Grand Rapids, Michigan: Eerdmans, 1996), 2.

[91] Oden, 32.

[92] Grenz, 7; Veith, 39.

constructs rationally designed systems In which humans find it impossible to live.[93]

Another possible starting point for the study of Postmodernism is the now famous quote from Jean Francois Lyotard: "simplifying to the extreme, I define Postmodern as incredulity towards metanarratives."[94] He started a revolution of thought that took academic circles by storm, filtering into every element of Western society through the graduates it produced.[95] Confronted with the emergence of a global culture and observing how the Enlightenment project was unsuccessful in bringing the desired utopia, postmodern ideas were quickly accepted and disseminated in every vein of society.

Recognizing the transitional nature of our time, and the lack of clarity which such transition brings, Anderson states that *Postmodern* is a makeshift word we use until we have decided what to name the baby.[96]

Characteristics of Postmodernism

The primary driving force behind the dawn of the Postmodern era is the attempt by philosophers and other intellectuals as well as societies to cope with the demise of the Modem dream on the one hand and the resultant need for another organizing principle for society at large. If technological and scientific advancement could not help us to live in peaceful coexistence, than what will?

---

[93] Veith, 39.

[94] Jean-Francois Lyotard, *The Postmodern Condition - a Report on Knowledge*, Translated by Geoff Bennington and Brian Massutni (Minneapolis, Minnesota: University of Minnesota Press, 1984), xxiv.

[95] Grenz, 39.

[96] Waiter Truett Anderson, The Truth about the Truth, (New York: Tacher Putnam Books, 1995), 3.

The answer to the question, Postmodernists hold, is to create a society in which there is room for everybody. And because it is our differing visions of truth that have historically divided us, the solution is to put less emphasis on our various versions of "the truth" and instead to respect each other's beliefs unequivocally. Such a view of life requires tolerance and respect from one individual to another, from one community to another, and from one society to another. This idea, called *Cultural Pluralism* (or sometimes just *Pluralism*), requires more than just tolerance for other practices and viewpoints: it affirms and celebrates diversity.[97] The more colorful it gets, the more we like it. Says Lesslie Newbigin: "Cultural pluralism I take to be the attitude which welcomes the variety of different cultures and life-styles within one society and believes that this is an enrichment to human life."[98]

However, Postmodernism is more than just a program of mutual respect and celebration of diversity; with it also comes the need to choose from a cultural smorgasbord of options and possibilities. As Jencks writes:

> The Post-Modern age is a time of incessant choosing. It's an era when no orthodoxy can be adopted without self-consciousness and irony, because all traditions seem to have some validity... the challenge is to choose and combine traditions selectively, to eclect (as the verb of eclecticism would have it) those aspects from the past and present which appear most relevant for the job at hand.[99]

---

[97] Grenz, 19.

[98] Lesslie Newbigin, *The Gospel in a Pluralist Society*, (Grand Rapids, Michigan: Eerdmans Publishing Company, 1989), 14.

[99] Charles Jencks, "What is Postmodernism" in *The Truth, about the Truth*, ed. Walter Truett Anderson (New York: Tacher Putnam Books, 1995), 57.

This tendency to combine elements of different worldviews and lifestyles has become increasingly visible in the church. Take for instance the example given by Leith Anderson of a young man who says he believes in Reformed theology, the inerrancy of Scripture ... and reincarnation.[100] Holding mutually contradictory ideas has become characteristic of the contemporary mind-set, says Veith. With no absolute canons of objective truth, the rational is replaced by the aesthetic. People tend to believe in what they like.[101]

Reduction of Absolute Truth to Relative Truth

Reducing truth to the realms of relativism may seem a purely pragmatic effort to create that society in which people of many convictions and lifestyles can coexist. The motivation to "not make a fuss over such things as personal beliefs and values" is rooted in a desire to "all get along." But on an academic level, and increasingly on every level of society, nothing could be further from the truth. To think that Postmodernists are purely pragmatic in relegating truth to the realms of relativism is naive. Postmodernism actively propagates the idea that there is no absolute truth and that all claims to truth are only well-crafted ideologies, designed on the one hand to give meaning to life, and, on the other hand, to also gain dominance over our environment.[102]

---

[100] Leith Anderson gave the example in a presentation, "Facing the Future," at the Evangelical Press Association Convention, St. Paul, Minnesota, 12 May 1993. The example was quoted by Veith, 175-76.

[101] Veith, 176.

[102] Op. Cit., 48. It is perhaps helpful to make a distinction here between philosophical Postmodernism, which often indeed tends to deny the existence of absolute truth, and cultural postmodernism, which sees absolute truth more as ultimately unknowable. See Brian McLaren, *Reinventing your Church* (Grand Rapids, Michigan: Zondervan, 1998), 173-174; McLaren proposes the idea that postmodern people actually have the understanding that truth, whatever it is, is too grand to put into propositional statements.

Postmodernists arrive at the conclusion that there is in fact no absolute truth from any direction. They argue, says Grenz, that we do not simply encounter a world that is "out there", but rather that we "construct" the world using concepts we bring to it.[103] This view of truth is called a Constructionist outlook, as opposed to the Objectivist outlook, which is the view that there is an objective world out there, which we can know through a process of investigation. There is no consensus as to whether or not there actually is an objective world out there. Some Postmodernists say there is, others that there isn't. In any case, it's immaterial, as we can never objectively know it! Veith summarizes this postmodern line of thinking well:

> Postmodern theories begin with the assumption that language cannot render truths about the world in an objective way. Language, by its very nature, shapes what we think. Since language is a social creation, meaning is (again) a social creation.[104]

Much of Postmodern thought starts with the study of linguistics, which has always noted that there was a distinction between "the signifier" (the word), and "the signified" (the meaning). The connection between the two is arbitrary, and the result of social agreement.[105]

This means that the meaning of words is a self-contained system. When you look up a word in the dictionary, you find more words. Words ultimately refer to other words. Much of our languages consist of abstractions

---

[103] Grenz, 41.

[104] Veith, 51.

[105] Almost all postmodern philosophers are deeply involved in the study of language. Nietzsche was a professor of philology, Derrida wrote extensively on linguistic issues (see his most well-known book, *Of Grammatology*, translated by Gayatri Chakravorty Spivak (Maryland, Baltimore: John Hopkins University Press, 1967).

that refer to nothing observable, but to mental (and thus, linguistic) concepts, writes Veith.[106] Consequently, Postmodernists have two basic assumptions. First, Postmodernists view all explanation of reality as constructions that are useful but not objectively true. Second, postmodernists deny that we have the ability to step outside our constructions of reality.[107]

This leads Steiner Kvale to the conclusion that language and knowledge do not copy reality. Rather, language constitutes reality, each language constructing specific aspects of reality in its own way.[108] The focus is on our interpretation, not on the reality that may or may not be out there.

In seeing things this way, postmodernists break with a concept of truth that has been around for a long time: the correspondence theory of truth.[109] This theory holds that truth and falsehood can be determined by simply comparing them to the real world. But as Postmodernists see that something can totally change simply by being re-described, they see that true and false are not determined by the real world, but by perspective. Walter Truett Anderson has a little story that best explains this view:

> Three umpires are sitting around over a beer, and one says, "There's balls and there's strikes, and I call 'em the way they are." Another says. "There's balls and there's strikes, and I call 'em the way I see 'em." The third says, "There's balls and there's strikes, and they ain't nothin' until I call em." Here we have an objectivist and two kinds

---

[106] Veith, 52.

[107] Grenz, 43.

[108] Steiner Kvale, "Themes of PostModernity" in *The Truth about the Truth*, ed. Walter Truett Anderson (New York: Tacher Putnam Books, 1995), 21.

[109] Grenz, 41.

of constructivists. The second umpire is what I would call a mainstream constructivist, the third a Postmodern radical.[110]

Since perspective determines perception, postmodernists look to the anthropologists to understand what determines perspective.[111] The answer is short: "myths." Anthropologists discovered that myths were more than ancient quaint stories about gods and goddesses, monsters and heroes. Myths in fact embody the central core of a culture's values and beliefs and are in that sense fundamentally religious. Further research led anthropologists to the conclusion that all societies, even Western ones, are bound together by a system of myths. Such a system of myths, writes Grenz, sustains the social relations within the society, and forms the basis of its claim to legitimacy. The Modern outlook claims to have replaced myths with rational postulates, but postmodern thinkers assert that the Enlightenment project is itself dependent on an appeal to narrative.[112]

Seeing that words describe everything, postmodernists see everything, every cultural artifact, as *text*. This explains the postmodern slogan: "the world is a text." Postmodernists see the world and everything in it as open for interpretation. Government, worldviews, technologies, histories, scientific theories, social customs, symbols, art and systems of faith are *all* essentially linguistic constructs, texts, or stories.[113]

---

[110] Anderson, 75.

[111] This is a clearly Nietzschean concept. Grenz observes: "There is no 'true world.' Everything is a "perspectival appearance" the origin of which lies within us. We live in a constructed world that comes from our own perspective. Grenz, 91.

[112] Grenz, 45.

[113] Veith, 52.

Such grand explanations that seek to explain (elements of) life and reality are also called *metanarratives* ~ stories about reality on a grand scale. While the intrinsic truth of such stories is questioned, or more accurately, denied, postmodernists view such stories as very important. They fulfill certain functions.

Explaining Human Experience

Metanarratives explain, sometimes in great detail, the "what" and "how" of our human experience. Whether one sees history as an eschatological process to the coming of a heavenly kingdom or an ever continuing process of evolution and survival of the fittest or perhaps the interplay of karma and circles of life, these worldviews are stories of a grand and metaphysical nature.

Meaning, Purpose and Values

In the explanations of the universe supplied to us by our metanarratives, we in turn find meaning. Metanarratives give meaning to life, at least at some levels. If our story is the ever continuing struggle of the oppressed against the oppressor, we will believe we exist to participate in that fight. If we think that life goes round and round until we have collected enough karma, we will live in pursuit of karma-building.

Whatever our story, it will give direction to our lives. Some metanarratives in this sense are more developed, particularly those that have been around longer. Besides giving meaning, metanarratives also give purpose. Because we act in accordance with what we believe, metanarratives direct our actions. With the people in our community we will engage in certain practices, and not others. Metanarratives also provide values. Sometimes these values are explicitly stated, such as the Ten Commandments.

Otherwise they are more implicit (i.e. survival of the fittest).

Group cohesiveness

Metanarratives also serve to preserve group cohesiveness. It helps us to distinguish between the "us" and the "not us". While metanarratives have all these positive functions, and they form highly complex systems that are fascinating to study to the sociologist and anthropologist, the actual content of the metanarrative is regarded with more than a little disbelief. It is for this reason that Jean Francois Lyotard expresses "incredulity towards metanarratives."[114]

Not only is there an *a priori* disbelief in any text; all texts are also suspiciously regarded as the source of much conflict. Because all human conflict starts with a difference of understanding, postmodernists believe that not stressing those differences, and not exalting one over another as being "more true," is the key to avoiding conflict.

However, postmodernists also see such texts as being essentially violent in nature. They are violent in that they are a tool of the community ruled by a specific metanarrative to gain control over others and mastery of their environment. Because no metanarrative has a complete hold on the truth, there are always individuals and areas of life that suffer at the hands of such a community.

This attitude is called "the hermeneutic of suspicion". Because postmodernists see the entire world as texts, which have great sociological and psychological value, but no intrinsic value, the question is asked how such texts then should be properly understood. Regarding them on the one side with a great deal of suspicion, while on the other hand regarding them also as potentially violent, postmodernists

---

[114] Lyotard, ibid.

answer that such texts should be understood with a great deal of suspicions. They approach texts not to ask what they *mean*, but what they *mask*.[115]

Destructing Ideologies and Language

While in evangelical eyes postmodernists can seem monolithic, the truth is that postmodernists vary one from another widely.[116] So-called Deconstructionism is not part and parcel of every postmodern agenda, and even interpretation of what Deconstructionism is, can vary. But while not characteristic of all postmodern thinkers, deconstructionism is one of postmodernism's more radical, and thus more well-known features. Deconstructionism seems to function on two levels. As we have seen, Postmodernists see language as the way we construct meaning. Language gives us words, words give us concepts, concepts give us worldviews, and worldviews only see so much. Language creates boundaries that we cannot step outside. It imposes limits and demands that we cannot escape. Our language determines the way we think, and what we think about. We cannot think in categories that our language does not give us words for, and we are thus limited to what our language allows. Consequently, postmodernists view language as a prison, and "they seek to undermine the walls so that we can break out."[117]

If language really does construct meaning (as opposed to an objective meaning already present in the world), then the work of the scholar is to take apart ("deconstruct") this meaning-

---

[115] Veith, 54.

[116] David Dockery lists four categories of Postmodernism: deconstructive, liberationist, constructive and conservative or restorationist. David Dockery, *The Challenge of Postmodernism - An Evangelical Engagement*, ed., David S. Dockery (Wheaton, Illinois: BridgePoint, 1995), 16.

[117] Veith, 53.

constructing process. By deconstructing influential concepts, perhaps we can break their control over our thoughts and actions.[118]

On the level of metanarrative, the role of Deconstructionism is to end the dominance of any one worldview over another and to bring freedom to every community with a metanarrative to deploy itself. Lesslie Newbigin understands this when he writes, "Part of the reason for the rejection of dogma is that it has for so long been entangled with coercion, with political power, and with the denial of freedom."[119]

Metanarratives are seen as "totalizing discourses", which are associated with oppression.[120] In the pursuit of the pluralistic society it is necessary to impose limits and bounds on those metanarratives that have historically threatened other meta-narratives. Because Christianity is perceived as having been one of the main oppressing forces, all sorts of efforts are now underway to attempt to contain Christianity's influence in society, and bring it back to an "acceptable" level.[121]

Postmodernism as Philosophy, Culture and Era

Those who pass off postmodernism as insignificant or inconsequential to Christians make the mistake of thinking that postmodernism is only a philosophy. After all, they wonder, aren't there many philosophies in the world?

---

[118] Grenz, 43.

[119] Newbigin, 10.

[120] Veith, 49.

[121] A good example of this in the USA would be the efforts of the ACLU, who are known for their efforts to reduce the amount of Christian influence in public life and culture. In Western societies many secular and humanist groups have similar aims.

Others mistake postmodernism for being just an expression of contemporary culture.

Yes, postmodernism is a philosophy. It has elaborate philosophical models and worldviews. It has its fair share of French writers (Jacques Derrida, Francois Lyotard, Michel Foucault), as well as many others (Chomsky, Rorty, Harvey, etc.). Nevertheless, Postmodern philosophy has been taught at universities across the world for a generation. And the academic world is not the ivory tower that it can seem to some, detached from the real world. That ivory tower indoctrinates the teachers, lawyers, journalists, and government officials.[122]

Through those channels, Postmodernism has become generally accepted into contemporary culture, or better yet, has come to form contemporary culture into what it is today. While for the average man or women living in the cities of Europe and America postmodernism may have lost some of its more aggressive and radical tenets, the basic sentiments are still staunchly defended.

A common misconception in the 1980s was to view postmodernism as synonymous with the so-called Grunge culture. The "Grunge Scene" originated in Seattle, Washington, was popularized by music groups such as Nirvana, and became very popular in almost every metropolitan city in the West. Indeed, Grunge had many postmodern features, and people in the Grunge scene no doubt tended to hold more to a Postmodern than Modern worldview. But postmodernism is more than just the Grunge Scene. It is a host-culture to all kinds of cultures. The Grunge Scene was a particular expression of youth culture. It found a spokesperson in Kurt Cobain, deceased lead singer of the Alternative rock music group *Nirvana*. But postmodernism has outlived Grunge, so it was a mistake to think postmodernism was merely a passing fad for trendy

---

[122] Veith, 162.

youth. The total impact of Postmodernism can only be properly understood if we understand it simultaneously as a culture, a philosophy, and an era.

A Culture

Every expression of culture is now experiencing the influence of Postmodernism. Our national cultures are no longer monolithic in their unity; instead, they are celebrations of diversity. The global culture has become a global melting-pot, and each of us has elements to add. Veith calls call this "a cosmic California."[123]

A Philosophy or Worldview

No major influence on Western thought and culture can be gained without strong philosophical underpinnings. This is provided by philosophers such as Nietzsche, Heidegger, Derrida, Foucault, Lyotard, Rorty, Chomsky, and many others. But while there is a host of philosophers whose names are usually mentioned in conjunction with Postmodernism, it is increasingly difficult to speak of a coherent philosophy of Postmodernism. Postmodernity has no set of practices and beliefs that gives it the coherence of classical Marxism, say, or Logical Positivism.[124]

A New era in Western thought

In the 1980s, the Postmodern worldview took the universities by storm. It influenced every aspect of culture and marked the transition away from that phase in Western history that we have called Modernity.

---

[123] Op. Cit., 50.

[124] Alan Padgett, "Christianity and Postmodernity," article published in *Christian Scholar's Review*, Volume XXVI, Number 2 (Winter 1996), *Special Issue: Christianity and PostModernity*, and also found at http://www.hope.eduiresources/csrAXVI2/padgett/

Postmodernism is best understood as a major development in Western thought. But Postmodernism, while perhaps a Western initiative, is very much a global phenomenon. It provides the overarching agenda for many of the efforts of the United Nations. From every part of the world we now see tribes and people groups coming forward and demanding their place. Much of the second and third world is trying to resist the dominant influence from the West, be it economic, cultural, religious, academic or political.

Postmodernism, Aristotle, and Plato

History can be dived in many different ways, and every way we divide it is of course a division we impose on it. We generally tend to think the Middle-Ages ended around 1500 AD, but no one woke up on Jan 1st, 1501 thinking this is an entirely new era. Life continued pretty much the same way for the vast majority as it always had.

A case can be made for dividing history into the following eras: the ancient world (everything up to 500); the Middle Ages (500-1500 AD), and the Modern period (1500 to ~ rather imprecisely, the latter decades of the twentieth-century). Of course, each era can be divided into several periods again.

As we have seen, most cultural observers view Postmodernism as the period that follows the age of Modernism. It is both a continuation from and a breaking away from that era and as such there are elements of both continuity and discontinuity. But some cultural observers and philosophers see an, even more, fundamental change taking place; the emergence of the Postmodern paradigm signifies a break with a way of thinking that has been present in Western thought for a long time. Since ancient Greece: Aristotle's law of non-contradiction, foundational to the concept of absolute truth, has fallen on hard times, says Gary Philips.[125] As a new era, Postmodernism signifies a transition from the Modern era, which has affected the West for more than two-hundred years. But in its denial of the Aristotelian view of truth, Postmodernism marks a change in some ways of thinking that have been fundamental to Western thought.

Isaiah Berlin comments further: Postmodernism denies three fundamental elements of Platonic wisdom that have been part of the Western mind for millennia.

First, Postmodernism denies that all questions have just one answer. Instead, Postmodernists hold that any question may have myriad answers, none of them better than another. No unbiased viewpoint exists that can in principle ensure agreements.[126]

Second, Postmodernism denies that there is a dependable path toward the truth. Because it denies the validity of the correspondence theory of truth (that all truths must necessarily resemble the real world), the best way to find out what is true is to assess the language we use, the concepts it affords us, and the way we use language to construct meaning. While we can discover meaning, there is no such thing as truth waiting out there to be discovered.

Third, Postmodernism denies that all the answers found in the quest for truth must be compatible with each other and fit into an organized whole, making one comprehensive system of truths that are coherent with one another. Aristotle's view of the coherence of truth is not very popular anymore. In the Postmodern world, people can hold to mutually conflicting truths, and never think

---

[125] Gary Philips, "Religious Pluralism in a Postmodern World," in *The Challenge of Postmodernism - An Evangelical Engagement*, ed., David S. Dockery (Wheaton, Illinois: BridgePoint, 1995), 261.

[126] Stanley Hauerwas, "Preaching as Though We Had Enemies," *First Things* 53, (May 1995).

twice about it.[127] What this demonstrates is that Postmodernism is not just a transition away from a Cartesian view of the world, but, and perhaps this, even more, significant, also a transition away from an Aristotelian/Platonic view of reality. If this is so, then Postmodernism may be the entrance door to a whole new era in human history.

Postmodernists have a sense that they are helping find the way into a new world; a world not beset by the challenges of the Modern and the Ancient world (though undoubtedly there are other challenges ahead - they do not expect a utopia any time soon), because of their advanced understanding of the nature of worldviews. The following best sums it up:

> The most astonishing thing of all, about man's fictions, is not that they have from prehistoric times hung like a flimsy canopy over his social world, but that he should have come to discover them at all. It is one of the most remarkable achievements of thought, of self-scrutiny, that the most anxiety-prone animal of all should come to see through himself and discover the fictional nature of his action world. Future historians will probably record it as one of the great, liberating breakthroughs of all time, and it happened in ours.[128]

Perhaps it is hard to believe in the significance of the time we live in. It is easy to downplay these transitions as hot air or sensationalism. This is understandable because few of us ever stop to consider *what* we believe let alone *how* we believe what we believe. And it is difficult to

---

[127] Isaiah Berlin, "The Idea of Pluralism," in *The Truth about the Truth*, ed. Walter Truett Anderson (New York: Tacher Putnam Books, 1995), 48.

[128] Ernest Becker, "The Fragile Fiction," in *The Truth about the Truth*, ed. Waiter Truett Anderson (New York: Tacher Putnam. Books, 1995), 35.

understand the nature of changes while one is going through them.[129] But Walter Truett Anderson tries to open our eyes a little bit when he says:

> Our everyday experience tends to be objectivist, guided by what the philosophers call 'naïve realism': we generally assume that the universe is the way we experience it. However, if asked to think about it, we turn into constructivists. Sure, we say, it's all relative; time and space and identity are subjective ideas - everybody knows that. Few of us realize that even to hold a concept of relative truth makes us entirely different from people who lived only a few decades ago.[130]

A New Expression of the Fall

As we saw at the end of chapter 1, Modernism, while it may be applauded in some of its pursuits, ultimately was a continuation of human rebellion against God. Man reigned supreme, and God was relegated to the margins of reality at best. Modernism was an expression of the human flight from God.

With the onset of the Postmodern era there is some discussion among some Christians concerning which of the two, Modernism or Postmodernism, is more biblical, more "right", even more Christian. Neither Modernism nor Postmodernism is our solution. Postmodernism is another phase in the flight from God. Like Modernism, Postmodernism is another human attempt to build a city, a global city this time, without God. In a way, the story of the tower of Babel is a continuing image of the effort of fallen man to regain a level of transcendence. Both Modernism and Postmodernism are new versions of the

---

[129] Anderson, *Reality Isn't What It Used To Be*, 2.

[130] Op. Cit., xii.

ancient tower of Babel, in that they are human endeavors to build a city with a tower that reaches to the heavens (the human desire for transcendence and spirituality without God), to make a name for themselves, so as not to be scattered in disarray.[131]

The truth of the matter is that God and His Word transcend any era, any culture, and any philosophy. Instead of looking for a city here on earth, Christians look for the heavenly city whose architect and builder is God.[132]

But while it is easy to reject Postmodernism because it is not the Kingdom of Heaven we are waiting for, we would do well to try and understand Postmodernism, such as it is, in order that we may effectively reach out to people. If we do, we will quickly be confronted with the pain, brokenness, and frustration caused by people's endeavors to live without God.

A transition, like the one we are seeing now, reveals some of the alienation, the desire for the sacred and the brokenness that is ours since the fall. The Postmodern cry for the community is a statement of loneliness. The New Age desire for spirituality is a longing for transcendence, coupled with the realization that a merely material existence offers no satisfaction. Postmodern philosophy, as dark as it may seem to some evangelicals, is an attempt to understand ourselves, and the world in which we live.

Generation X: a Postmodern Generation

Much has been written in the past decades about Generation X, the emerging generation of young people now making their way in the world. Various authors have attempted to describe Generation X, listing defining characteristics. While a general picture does emerge over what constitutes and defines Generation X, there is also

---

[131] Genesis 11:4.

[132] Hebrews 11:10,16.

much discrepancy. One of the main areas of disagreement is over the years of birth that mark this generation. Zander points to 1965 and 1980 as the years between which Generation X was born.[133] Barna puts it from 1965 and 1983.[134] And Tapia puts it from 1963 and 1977.[135] Thus the widest band (at the time of writing) puts this generation in the 33-53 age-bracket. But what about people who fall outside this category, especially those in their twenties ~ are they influenced by Postmodernism?

Do dates really define Generation X? Most experts would agree that Generation X is defined by worldview rather than dates. As Kevin Ford says:

> Mindset and worldview are more important than arbitrary dates, however. You might meet a Boomer who was born in '65, and a Buster who was born in '61. In fact, those transitional years of the early sixties undoubtedly produced a few hybrid varieties of thirty-somethings who show characteristics of both generations.[136]

In pointing to worldview and mindset, Ford refers to the Postmodern Ethos and Tapia agrees:

> The young men and women who make up Generation X are as diverse in outlook and style as the baby boomers before them. But what makes Generation X unique is the spirit of their age - an

---

[133] Dieter Zander, "Reaching the Busters: One Church's Experience," *Lead On*, Spring 1994, 8.

[134] George Barna, "The Invisible Generation: Baby Busters" (Glendale, California: Barna Research Group, 1992), 20.

[135] Andres Tapia, "Generation X", *Christianity Today* (September 12, 1994), 18.

[136] Kevin Ford, "Generation X My Generation", (Intervarsity, Winter 1994-95), 3.

age widely regarded as Postmodern and often as post-Christian.[137]

And:

The distinctive nature of Generation X results not only from massive changes within American society, but also from a paradigm shift in Western culture the transition from Modernism (the Enlightenment's legacy) to post-Modernism (a radical reaction against the Enlightenment understanding of truth).

Generation X is the first generation to grow up amidst this Postmodern world-view. To know Generation X, it is important to understand two competing paradigms—one exemplified by the apologetic style of Josh McDowell's book Evidence That Demands a Verdict; the other by MTV.[138]

Todd Hahn says, "The overwhelming majority of Baby Busters do not believe in absolute truth. This concept of truth has shaped this generation's worldview."[139] Jimmy Long agrees: Generation X is the first purely Postmodern generation.[140] That Generation X is thoroughly familiar with the Postmodern world and the Postmodern way of thinking becomes clear:

> In Postmodern Orthodoxy, we are taking for granted the achievements of Modernity, of Modern methods of inquiry, Modern procedures of searching scientifically for truth, and Modern assumptions for a just democratic political order.

---

[137] Tapia, ibid.

[138] Ibid.

[139] Todd Hahn and David Verhaagen, Reckless Hope - Understanding and Reaching Baby-Busters (Grand Rapids, Michigan: Baker Book House, 1996), 39.

[140] Jimmy Long, Generating Hope - A Strategy for Reaching the Postmodern Generation (Downer's Grove, Illinois: InterVarsity Press, 1997), 52.

The problem my young fogey friends experience is not that they are yet to be introduced to these agendas. They have already been through these agendas *ad nauseam*...These young people have been hardened by Modernity to use the methods of Modern inquiry (the methods of psychological analysis, sociological, political, historical analysis, scientific and literary analysis) to detoxify the illusions of Modernity.[141]

Generation X seems to be more of an American phenomenon: the same distinctions between Generation X and their predecessors cannot be observed as easily in Europe or elsewhere. This is because in Europe the societal transition from Modernism to Postmodernism has been going on far longer, and has consequently had more time to have its effect to a much deeper level than in America.

However, if this is so, then Europe can be a case-study for American evangelicals desiring to understand and engage with Postmodern culture. The European scene may be a foretaste of what the U.S. should expect. To aid this process of comparing Europe and the U.S., it is probably best to ignore the term Generation X, and instead to speak of "Postmodern people" ~ people with a Postmodern outlook on life. This would offer some advantages.

First, it allows authors and speakers on the subject to focus on the essential, not the details. The essence of the problem is how to interact with people who approach the world with a Postmodern mindset. In that discussion it is worldview that matters, not so much dates of birth.

Second, the rest of society does not make as much of Generation X as the church has done. Nearly half of all publications on Generation X have been published within

---

[141] Oden, "The Death of Modernity and Postmodern Evangelical Spirituality," in *The Challenge of Postmodernism - An Evangelical Engagement*, 20-21.

evangelical circles, making the concept sometimes somewhat distorted. To speak of Postmodern people, however, is far more accepted, now that Postmodernism is a recognized term across all academic circles, frequently utilized by the media.

Third, one can compare the situation between Europe, Australia, New Zealand and the U.S.

Postmodernism and Evangelicalism

Evangelicals were divided in their response to the advent of the Postmodern era. Evangelical thinkers like Oden, Pinnock, Walsh, Middleton and Walter Brueggeman regard the Postmodern condition as favorable for Christian faith, Others, like Veith, Wells, Henry and McCallum regard Postmodernism often with suspicion, if not outright rejection.

The first group does not embrace all of Postmodern thinking and culture. In fact, for some, there is very little to embrace. But there is often a clear agreement with the Postmodern critique of Modernism. There is among them an awareness that the Postmodern environment is much more conducive to the gospel, and that some of its values correspond to biblical values. While the people in this group understand that Postmodernism is not the Kingdom of God, they look at the Postmodern era as one of new opportunity, an era bringing new ways of communicating the gospel. Scott Moore is representative of this group:

> I believe that Christian intellectuals have much to celebrate in the cultural-intellectual *turn* which is postmodernity. The turn [from Modernism to Postmodernism] is dangerous because we do not know what lies ahead, and in our usual arrogance, we're probably taking it too quickly. What is wonderful and exciting is that new vistas and insights confront us at every turn. We are no

longer constrained only to see the facts of the world in the ways that our larger non-Christian, Modern culture has demanded. In truth, we have new vantage points from which to view the notion of "facts" at all. And this is the first point we Christian intellectuals have to celebrate about the Postmodern turn.[142]

The second group often critiques Postmodernism on two grounds. First, they find that Postmodernism is not biblical. Second, they critique Postmodernism with Modern arguments. Unhappy with the turn of events and developments in recent years, they display a reticence to move forward, if not a clear desire to return to "the good old days." Having been attacked for three hundred years because of their belief in the supernatural, many evangelicals now have an attitude which is both deeply defensive and profoundly conservative.[143]

To better understand the tension between evangelicalism and Postmodernism, it is necessary to understand the relationship between a religion and its surrounding society. James Hunter suggests three ways in which a community of faith responds to Modernity: *withdrawal, accommodation and resistance.*[144] *Withdrawal* is the strategy chosen to minimize contact with the Modern world. As an example of this, Hunter mentions the Amish community. *Accommodation* is a conscious embrace of norms and values from the Modern world. This has been

---

[142] Scott H. Moore, "Era and Epoch, Epoch and Era: Christian Intellectuals in the Postmodern Turn," article published in *Christian Scholar's Review*, Volume XXVI, Number 2 (Winter 1996), Special Issue: Christianity and PostModernity.

[143] J. Bottum, "Christians and Postmoderns." In *First Things*, 40 (February 1994), 28-32.

[144] Hunter, "What is Modernity? Historical Roots and Contemporary Features," in *Faith and Modernity*, ed. Philip Sampson, Vinay Samuel and Chris Sugden (Oxford, United Kingdom: Regnum Books, 1994), 22.

the option chosen by what has since become known as the liberal theologians. *Resistance* is the choice to engage the Modern world while trying to resist its secularizing influence. This is traditionally the option chosen by evangelicals.

Evangelicalism shares close ties with Modernity. A child of the Reformation, pietism, and revivalism, the evangelical movement was born in the early Modern period. And North American Evangelicalism reached maturity in the mid-twentieth century - at the height of the Modern era. As Modern thinkers, evangelicals have always used the tools of Modernity, such as the scientific method, the empirical approach to reality, and common sense realism. But these tools became especially important in the 20th century, as evangelical intellectuals attempted to understand and articulate the gospel with eyes turned toward the challenge posed by the worldview of late Modernity - secularism.[145]

Hunter further explains the relationship between evangelicalism and Modernism:

> It is impossible to engage the Modern without being subtly changed. Orthodoxy becomes something other than what earlier (premodern) generations of orthodox believers believed and practiced...In sum, the meaning of faith undergoes subtle but significant changes in the context of Modernity.[146]

The influence of Modernity on evangelical faith is becoming clearer as Christian traditions from elsewhere raise their voices. Hesselgrave told of fifty-five delegates (and thirty-five observers) ~ all conservative evangelicals ~ from Asia, Africa, Latin America, the Caribbean, and the Pacific Islands, who met in Seoul, Korea, in 1982. Calling

---

[145] Grenz, 161.

[146] Hunter, 23, 26.

attention to the "theological captivity" of the church in their parts of the world, they issued what is known as the Seoul Declaration. In it they highlighted the limitations of Western theology as seen from their non-Western points of view. Among those limitations are the following:

1. Western theology is, by and large, rationalistic, and preoccupied with intellectual concerns, especially those having to do with faith and reason.

2. It is molded by Western philosophies.

3. It has consciously been conformed to the secularistic worldview associated with the Enlightenment. It is captivated by Western Individualism.[147]

One can perhaps not blame the apologists of the eighteenth and nineteenth centuries for fighting their battles with liberal theology with the same weapons as their perceived opponents. They staunchly defended Christianity from the attacks of anti-supernaturalism (naturalism) seeking to be credible to a world drifting away from God. Stanley Hauerwas says Christians in Modernity thought their task was to make the gospel intelligible to the world rather than to help the world understand why it could not be intelligible without the gospel.[148]

While it is understandable that evangelicals took on some Modern features, these dynamics are now becoming evident as the Modern worldview gives way to the Postmodern worldview.

Lesslie Newbigin writes:

---

[147] David J. Hesselgrave, *Communicating Christ Cross-Culturally - an Introduction to Missionary Communication*, 2d ed. (Grand Rapids, Michigan: Zondervan, 1991), 203-204. Hesselgrave is quoting from: "Seoul Declaration: Toward an Evangelical Theology for the Third World," in Bong Rin Ro and Ruth Eshenauer, eds, *The Bible and Theology in Asian Contexts*, (Taichung, Taiwan: Asian Theological Association, 1984), 23.

[148] Stanley Hauerwas, "Preaching as Though We Had Enemies," *First Things* 53, (May 1995).

What is striking about the books which were written...to defend Christianity against these attacks, is the degree to which they accept the assumptions of their assailants. Christianity is defended as being reasonable...There is little suggestion that the assumptions themselves are to be challenged. The defense is in fact a tactical retreat.[149]

Doug Irwin references some examples of this in a paper on rationalist apologetics in the Postmodern era:

Back in the seventies, one of the popular selling books among evangelical Christians was Josh McDowell's, *Evidence that Demands a Verdict.*[150] This book was a collection of persuasive arguments used to arm Christians in their evangelistic pursuits with their skeptical friends. It typified the kind of approach that was my experience in evangelistic training and evangelistic preaching during my growing up years. Evangelism Explosion[151] gave a neat, well-ordered strategy for "cold-turkey" witnessing. Word of Life, a conservative evangelical youth ministry I was involved in, packaged the gospel in 20 minute presentations with an urgent call to respond immediately to the message of the gospel just shared. Campus Crusade armed students with *The Four Spiritual Laws* tract, charging them to take people through the booklet and call for a decision.

What do all these evangelistic approaches have in common? My assessment would categorize

---

[149] Newbigin, 3.

[150] Josh McDowell, *Evidence that Demands a Verdict* (San Bernardino, California: Here's Life Publishers, 1972).

[151] D. James Kennedy, *Evangelism Explosion* (Wheaton, Illinois: Tyndale House Publishers, 1970).

these evangelistic strategies as a "Modern" approach to evangelism. This style of evangelism has certain characteristics that suit itself well to the Modern mindset. First, it assumes there are rational, objective, absolute truths. This form of communication presupposes that the listener holds to a Modern epistemology, namely that there are absolute self-existent truths out there which need to be discovered and embraced." Second, this kind of witnessing assumes a common recognition of the laws of logic and reasoning. Not to minimize the work of the Holy Spirit in the conversion of an unbeliever, but such approaches imply that the most effective means of sharing Christ is through propositional truth statements, which logically lead someone to conclude that accepting Christ as Savior is the best (perhaps, only) course of action. Of course, this assumes that the person we are witnessing to exercises faith in response to logical reasoning - a position more consistent with a Modern epistemological view, than Postmodern. Third, it assumes people have a "discovery" notion of belief. By this, I mean that people recognize that meaning and truth is existent outside themselves, and their goal in pursuing the meaning of life is to search for it until they have found it. Such a frame of reference can make them a good candidate for listening to a gospel presentation as the Holy Spirit works on their heart, but if their notion of truth changes to reject a self-existent concept of truth external to who they are, then they are less likely to be open to an outside witness.

Given the assumptions of a rational apologetic witness, it won't be difficult to see how this approach to evangelism becomes less persuasive in a growing Postmodern society.[152]

Newbigin goes on to state that "it is plain that that we do not defend the Christian message by domesticating it within the reigning plausibility structure. That was surely the grand mistake of the eighteenth-century defenses of the reasonableness of Christianity."[153] Scott Moore concurs:

> However, what is so special about postmodernity? Haven't intelligent Christians been saying these sorts of things [about the nature of truth] all along? Well, yes and no. For a very long time (about 1700 years) Christians said things like this, but for the last 300 years or so, most of us have desperately wanted to validate our knowledge claims by the methods and assumptions of the reigning knowledge people in our culture. Lately, that's been the scientists. They liked to talk about the results of their inquiries as being "objective." The things they were describing were "objects" out there in the world, not the distortive, subjective interests of the investigators. Real truth became objective truth...
>
> The Christian narrative never claimed any of those kinds of things, and it was only because we desperately wanted to be paid Modernity's compliment that we tied Christian truth to notions of objective fact.[154]

---

[152] Doug Irwin, "In Search of a Postmodern Apologetic" (paper) given at D. A. Carson conference at Trinity Evangelical Divinity School, Deerfield, Illinois, April 1997.

[153] Newbigin, 10

[154] Moore, ibid.

This leads us to the conclusion that, while Evangelicalism sought to uphold Orthodox Christian faith in the Modem world, Modernism in fact had a profound effect on Evangelicalism. On the basis of the above, it is fair to say that Christianity was, in fact, Modernized, in the sense that some of Modernity's presuppositions and attitudes became an intrinsic part of Evangelicalism.

However, if that is so, it is no small wonder that many evangelicals now feel at odds with Postmodernism, and are sometimes prone to critique it not on the basis of biblical arguments, but rather on the basis of Modern ones. Unaware of the extent to which their belief structure has been influenced by Modernism, they now critique Postmodernism with arguments more reminiscent of Descartes and Newton than of Paul and Peter.

People in this second group have adopted a very skeptical approach towards Postmodernism. If Modernism was dark, Postmodernism is far darker still. This turn of events is unfortunate, and some seize every opportunity to lament it. Within this group Merold Westphal has identified two sub-groups ~ those who hope that "this negative French stuff" will soon go away, and who have, as he calls it, adopted an ostrich mentality, sticking their head in the sand. Secondly, Westphal identifies those who view Postmodernism as the new "bogeyman." Here Postmodern criticism becomes demonized as those atheistic, un-biblical thinkers.[155] Dennis McCallum is perhaps a representative of this group when he writes: "Most of Postmodernism defies every canon of common sense and every law of rationality." He then goes on to describe Postmodernism as nihilistic, dogmatic and oppressive; in short a turn for the worse.[156] Another example is Veith, who, at the conclusion

---

[155] Merold Westphal as quoted by Alan Padgett, ibid.

[156] Dennis McCallum, "The Real Issue - The Postmodern Puzzle - When there are no absolute truths and no rules of logic, how do we defend the gospel?",

of his book, lists eight characteristics of Postmodernism to demonstrate that it is militant, anti-rational, anti-foundational, reactionary, anti-Christian, anti-democratic, anti-individual, anti-transcendence and revolutionary in nature. It is clear that Veith views Postmodernism as dangerous, and that he finds very little there that is attractive or helpful.

Where Do We Go from Here?

How then should evangelicals go on? Different people give different answers. There are those who would like to go back to the pre-Modem era, arguing that essentially Christianity was at its purest in the first few centuries. Most noticeable among these is Thomas Oden, who suggests that the first six centuries of Christianity provide all the inspiration we need for life in ministry in our time.[157] An example of this is His *Pastoral Theology*, which is an exposition of writings of the Church Fathers of the first six centuries on the responsibilities and lives of those in ministry.[158]

Then there are those who would like to return to the Modern era. There is a sense that evangelicalism was a powerful movement in the Modem era, and some experience a sense of loss and frustration that evangelicalism is slowly losing relevance in society.

And there are those who look forward with hope, and perhaps even with celebration. Here Alan Padgett makes a helpful distinction as he discerns two groups. On the one

---

an excerpt from *The Death of Truth* (Bethany House Publishers, 1996), Chapter 15, and found at http://www.leaderu.corn/reaUri9802/mccallum.html

[157] See Thomas Oden, After Modernity...What? *Agenda for Theology* (Grand Rapids, Michigan: Zondervan Publishing House, 1992). Oden calls his position "Liberated Orthodoxy" (p. 149).

[158] Thomas Oden, *Pastoral Theology* (San Francisco: Harper and Row, 1982).

hand there those who have a "best buddy" view of Postmodernism. In this approach there is very little critical appraisal of Postmodernism. On the other hand Padgett sees those who see Postmodernism as a critical dialogue partner. This is Padgett's choice:

> Here we listen to the concerns of the Postmodern attitude and address ourselves to this audience, rather than demonizing them or hoping they will go away. We are willing to admit that Christianity in the past bought into a "God of the philosophers" that was part of an onto-theo-logical project which objectified the Other and the ecosystem, leading to social and physical violence to them both. We should study the best Postmodern thinkers carefully and pay attention to their insights.[159]

He continues:

> I don't think the way forward is the way back to pre-Modernism nor to defend Modernity. Christianity must pass through both the acids of Modernity and the suspicion and negativity of post-Modernity into its own healthy self-conception of self-in-community-with-the-Other. This healthy self-conception in community will focus especially on God as Other but will also include Neighbor and Fellow-Creature as Others.[160]

---

[159] Padgett, ibid.

[160] Ibid.

CHAPTER 4 Constants In Changing Times

The emergence of the Postmodern era sometimes seems to go together with the desire to jettison everything that we had in the Modern era. While no doubt there are some Postmodernists for whom this is true, as Christians we need to realize that neither the Modern nor the Postmodern world is our home, and we should be wary of becoming too comfortable in either one.

Realizing that we belong neither to the Modern nor the Postmodern era, we can observe both from a slight distance and perceive both the merits and shortfalls of each era. I say "from a slight distance" because our humanness does not allow us to disengage fully from either worldview. To some extent, we will always (at least while in this body) be conditioned by the worldview of the world in which we grow up. Our observation is always that of the participant, not that of the neutral distant, impartial and unaffected observer.

As our world turned from the Modern era into the Postmodern era, Christians experienced much upheaval. But as the dust settled we learned that there are still things we can hold on to ~ the constants ~ those things that are unaffected by the transition from Modernism to Postmodernism, and which can be affirmed in both eras.

The primacy of Evangelism

Modern people needed Christ because he was absent from their worldview. It had taken some time before we understood that the Modern worldview was incompatible with the Christian faith. While people like Descartes, Pascal and Newton, whose work was foundational to the Modern worldview, themselves were "Christians", over time God was more and more relegated to the margins of our worldview, until Darwin's Origin of the Species allowed Modern people to dispense with the idea of God. It was only over time that it became apparent that Modernism was a worldview with no room for God, and it took a little longer still before Christians realized that the light of the gospel was needed wherever the worldview of Modernism was held. This delay is understandable given the fact that the West moved from a Christian worldview to an atheistic or at least agnostic worldview rather slowly and imperceptibly at first. Christians were, understandably, unaware and unprepared for the emerging world around them that was abandoning faith in God. Gradually and eventually they caught up.

At the same time, exploration of the seas and colonization brought us in contact with peoples and cultures that had no knowledge of the Christian gospel. In this context, this is how missions came to be understood: chunks of the "pagan" world outside Europe had to be conquered and incorporated into Christendom. Contact with non-Christian cultures soon gave rise to what became a powerful missionary movement, which sent missionaries to almost every place under the sun.

In addition, as the attention went to missionary efforts in faraway places, few (initially at least) noticed that back home in Europe people started turning away from God and faith by the thousands. Convinced of a worldview that had no need for God and that boosted confidence in human ability to master anything; the West became increasingly secularized. When it became clear that the church also had to do something about the growing numbers of Westerners who had, practically, turned their backs on the Christian faith, this enterprise was referred to as "home missions."[161]

"Foreign Missions", the endeavor to convert pagan people in far-off lands to the Christian faith, was seen in a

---

[161] Ibid.

different light to "home-missions," the endeavor to attract people back to the church. Much of the effort that went into home-missions went into diaconal work, rather than "reconversion".[162]

> Gradually, however, a change of terminology was introduced: "mission" was now only used in respect of work in traditional "non-Christian" countries. Reconversion work in the West was referred to as "evangelism" (or "evangelization"). The latter was judged to be theologically different from the former.[163]

And so, a distinction was made between missions and evangelism. While the Western church went to great lengths to engage in mission by sending missionaries and resources, not nearly as much effort was made to engage in evangelism at the home-front. "This view, that mission and evangelism are theologically different, is still widely held and it is usually linked to the view that "mission" out there is more important than "evangelism" here in the West.[164]

Consequently, little effort was made to actively reach people that were becoming increasingly secularized. The awareness that the West was once again a Mission-field is relatively new:

> As late as 1943 - when Grodin and Daniel published their *France, pays de mission?* in which they argued that France, the eldest daughter of the Church, had once again become a mission-field and that a missionary effort ... verseas was called

---

[162] Of course a person can only be converted once but my meaning here is different.

[163] Ibid.

[164] Op. Cit., 30.

for ~ their reflections were greeted with shock rather than an endorsement.[165]

The post-war climate started changing that. Increasingly Christians found it impossible to refer to their culture as "Christian". With the realization that the process of secularization was impacting society in Europe and the United States came the gradual understanding that the West was home to "neo-pagans", and that the dichotomy between the religious landscape in for instance Africa on the one side, and the West on the other, was in fact false.

And yet, even today some Christians seem content to maintain merely the status quo. Some churches lack the motivation to engage actively non-Christians in the hope of seeing them enter the Kingdom for which Jesus died. While the fields may be white for harvest, the workers are sitting in the church pews, or, at best, on the barricades of such enclaves, desperately trying to stop a tsunami that is washing away every memory of a Christian past.

The dichotomy between missions and evangelism and the emphasis the first has received over the latter, has resulted in the loss of a correct understanding of the nature of the church. Too long missions and evangelism have been seen as an adjunct activity of the Church, "in this definition, then, missions continue to belong to the *adiaphora* (ἀδιάφορα), not to the essence of the church...It remains peripheral, just as the discipline of missiology remains peripheral, in Western institutions: only those interested in "overseas" work or in exotic theologies take these courses.[166]

This dichotomy is unfortunate, in that it makes missions and evangelism merely one function of the church and does

---

[165] Op. Cit., 31.

[166] Op. Cit., 32.

not define them as essential, as being part of the essence of the church.

> This is, however, decidedly not what mission is and what missiology should be involved in ... Mission refers to a permanent and intrinsic dimension of the church's life...it is impossible to talk about church without at the same talking about mission. Because God is a missionary God, God's people are a missionary people.[167]

Mission and evangelism then should be understood as one and the same thing, and they are at the core of what the church is all about.

Why is this important to our discussion of Postmodernism? As we have seen Modernism as a worldview turned out to have little in common with the Christian worldview, and it appears that the Postmodern worldview is no more Christian. This means that in those parts of the world where the Modern or Postmodern worldviews are dominant, many people, in fact, live in spiritual darkness. With all the best intentions possible, it is impossible to refer seriously to Europe as a Christian continent. In the U.S., one can still discern a strong Christian tradition, but there also Postmodernism is rapidly taking over as the dominant cultural influence and worldview, and the distinctions are getting stronger.

The Need for Contextualization

Having established the need to reach Postmodern people for Christ, the question immediately arises: but how?' Many evangelicals, in fact, do feel like they cannot relate to Postmodern people. For many of them, trying to reach Postmoderns is, in fact, going to be a cross-cultural experience.

---

[167] Ibid.

The need for contextualization is well expressed in the opening paragraph of the preface to Hesselgrave and Rommen's book *Contextualization*:

> Undergirding this book is a simple thesis: namely, contextualization is more than a neologism, it is a necessity. Of course, this thesis rests on certain presuppositions. First, it is imperative that the Great Commission be fulfilled and the world be evangelized. Second, however, world evangelization is defined, at the very least it entails an understandable hearing of the gospel. Third, if the gospel is to be understood, contextualization must be true to the complete authority and unadulterated message of the Bible on the one hand, and it must be related to the cultural, linguistic, and religious background of the respondents on the other.[168]

Postmoderns, like the Moderns before them, need the gospel contextualized for them in order to be able to understand it. It is important that we as Christians do not remain stuck in the Modern age; while we may differ in the degree to which we like the Postmodern worldview, it is important that we learn to understand it, and how to reach out to the people in it.

The Authority of Scripture

The Word of God tells us to live in the Postmodern age, to worship God in the Postmodern age, to evangelize in the Postmodern age, and to live lives that are pleasing to him in the Postmodern age. While the Bible may never name the Postmodern age, it is clear from the Bible that ages will come and go, but that God's Word remains the

---

[168] David J. Hesseigrave and Edward Rommen, *Contextualization - Meanings, Methods and Models* (Grand Rapids, Michigan: Baker Book House, 1989), xi.

same (Isa. 40:8). However, like in the Modern age, the authority of Scripture is under attack in the Postmodern age. Carson points out that "it is not surprising that...skepticism about the Bible is one of the leading factors contributing to the rise of religious pluralism and the rejection of exclusivism."[169] And yet, because God has clearly chosen Scripture as the means by which he is revealing himself in the twenty-first century, we cannot afford to treat Scripture like we would a buffet, picking and choosing what we like and what suits our needs and desires while leaving the rest. What God has disclosed of himself in Scripture does not permit us to pick and choose.

While Carson, who equates pluralism with Postmodernism, and sees little good in either one, holds to a high view of the authority of the Bible, he also realizes that biblical criticism of the last few decades has brought some good insights, and that a purely propositional reading, which is basically a Modern approach to the text, is no longer an option either.

> Scripture boasts many communicative acts: history, letter, proverbs, wisdom utterances, warnings, songs, questions, discourse, diatribes, gematria, apocalyptic, legal codes, moral exhortation, threats, promises, commands, laments and so on. Some of these are recognized and recognizable genres; others are admittedly genres, but with fuzzy borders. Some are genres found within several other genres. And genres typically have their own interpretive "rules," learned by observation and practice.[170]

Then Carson cites Gerhart, "Remembering this will provide the needed correction to propositional and

---

[169] D.A Carson, *The Gagging of God* (Grand Rapids, Michigan: Zondervan, 1996), 151.

[170] Op. Cit., 189.

metaphorical theology alike: the Bible does not merely give us atomistic propositions about God, nor free-floating metaphors, but ways of processing and organizing propositions and metaphors into meaningful wholes."[171]

If we can learn that, then perhaps we have moved beyond a simplistic Modernist reading of the Bible and seeking to translate it into propositions, and that perhaps Postmodernism, with its respect for other cultures, has taught us something about biblical interpretation. There is, of course, a strong tension between the evangelical view of the Scriptures, which holds that the Scriptures are authoritative because they were divinely inspired, and the postmodern hermeneutic, which says that the only thing that matters is not what the author was trying to say, but how the reader understands and responds to the text.[172]

The Need for Reason

To some Christians Postmodernism seems little more than a plea to stop using our God-given ability to think. It seems to them that Postmodernism is a simple appeal to jettison all rational endeavors, and abandon ourselves to irrationality, with insanity not too far beyond that.

There is some truth in this; indeed, there are Postmodernists (most noticeably Deconstructionists) who believe that all reason is merely a bid for power. However, to view Postmodernism in such a restricted sense is throwing out the baby with the bath-water. Mainstream Postmodernism, or Postmodernism as it works in contemporary culture, sees a definite place for reason;

---

[171] Op. Cit., 190; quoting from Mary Gerhart, "Generic Competence in Biblical Hermeneutics" *Semeia* 43 (1988), 40.

[172] For more information on the subjects of hermeneutical method see: D.A Carson, *The Gagging of God* (Grand Rapids, Michigan: Zondervan, 1996) and Alistair McGrath, *A Passion for Truth - The Intellectual Coherence of Evangelicalism* (Downers Grove, Illinois: Intervarsity Press, 1996).

reason just does not reign supreme anymore. Rather than abandoning reason, other ways of knowing are explored alongside reason. Grenz Says, "In Postmodernism, the primary assumption is that truth is not rational or objective...There are other ways of knowing, including one's emotions and intuition."[173]

The average Postmodern person seeks to balance properly all ways of knowing, hoping to gain thereby maximum yield of information. This desire for holism is a reaction against the Modern emphasis on reason at the expense of emotion, spirituality and community.

The X-Files

An example of this was evident in the popular TV-series, *The X-Files*, aired from 1993 to 2002. In this series, two FBI agents, Scully, and Mulder, investigate strange phenomena and crimes, including extra-terrestrial life, government-conspiracies, religious oddities, paranormal gifting, etc. The underlying theme of the show is the attempt of the two central characters to understand the crime/phenomenon. Scully is a Medical Doctor, and invariably approaches things from a rational perspective, always with strong doubt about anything supernatural or extraordinary. Mulder, on the other hand, has a much more open mind, always seeking to get to the heart of the matter by any means necessary. Episodes frequently ended with a brief personal comment by either Scully or Mulder, something along the lines of "I used to think that...but now I understand that...and perhaps one day..." displaying humility before truth.

The motto of the show was "The Truth is out there" and the show demonstrated a belief that there is truth, but that we can only ever try to approximate it, never quite

---

[173] Stanley Grenz, as quoted by Andres Tapia, "Generation X", *Christianity Today* (September 12, 1994), 18.

totally find it. In the pursuit of truth, any means of gathering information is valid: The *modus operandi*, in true Postmodern fashion is: "Whatever works."

Postmodern people, then, do not jettison all reason; they simply complement reason with other ways of perception. The implication for Christian apologetics is that appeals to reason and appeals on the basis of reason can still be made; they should simply be complemented by strategies that seek to target these other ways of perception.

Challenged by the perspectives of the Postmodern era the evangelical landscape is changing. The insights that our reasoning abilities are both fallible and fallen, that there are more ways to knowing (and believing) than pure reasoning, and that God created us with a number of faculties instead of just the one, have created a hunger to explore those other faculties. This hunger has resulted in a strong and steady flow of books on such topics as inner-healing, counseling, meditation, deeper-spirituality, spiritual disciplines, etc. Evangelicals are shaking off their Modernist preoccupation with reason, and this is influencing our evangelistic strategies.

That is a good thing. As long as reason and reasonability are the chief aspects of our apologetic, we will continue to be irrelevant to Postmodern people. We may think we are relevant, simply because we have "the truth" but they will simply not give us the time of day. One person who seems to grasp strongly this point is Lesslie Newbigin:

> Lesslie Newbigin will not begin, bowing and scraping in the traditional way, by commending Christianity as a reasonable faith. That, he thinks, would abandon the climb before the first pitch. Reasonable by whose standards? The gospel cannot be "proved," he says, because that would presuppose a truth more fundamental than the gospel, by which the gospel can be proved. To

him, the gospel story is the central and most fundamental of all truths. "The proper form of apologetics is the preaching of the gospel itself and the demonstration ~ which is not merely or primarily a matter of words--that it does provide the best foundation for a way of grasping and dealing with the mystery of our existence in this universe."[174]

The Power of the Gospel

In the midst of socio-cultural change, it seems like many Christians have given in to an overriding pessimism that "it's all going downhill." A feeling of "we are the last of the good guys" seems to be predominant in many Christian circles. The attitude is one of "holding on to all that we've got." This besieged mentality is evident with Carl Henry, "Nightfall for Western civilization is close at hand. Let me leave no doubt then about my deep conviction. As I see it, the believing church is the West's last and only real bastion against barbarism."[175]

The *modus operandi* to be successful as such a bastion seems to be the use of the political system. More and more Christians, particularly in America, are seeking to use political means to make their presence known, and to function as a voice for conservatism. Jimmy Long calls this attitude the battling church, and laments its effect in the long run:[176]

---

[174] Tim Stafford, "God's Missionary to Us," *Christianity Today*, 40 (December 9, 1996), 24.

[175] Jimmy Long, *Generating Hope - A Strategy for Reaching the Postmodern Generation* (Downer's Grove, Illinois: InterVarsity Press, 1997), 23.

[176] Long discusses five perspectives on the church: the assimilating church, the protecting church, the unchanging church, the battling church and the influencing church (pp. 18-35). His categories are an adaptation of H. Richard Niebuhr, *Christ and Culture* (New York: Harper and Row, 1951).

I can envision the battling church, as represented by the Christian Coalition, winning the culture war in the short time but losing the battle for the souls of Generation X and coming postmodern generations. They will have spent so much time winning political wars that they will have neglected the spiritual battle for people's souls.[177]

Unfortunately, Christians have positioned themselves opposite each other in their disagreement over how they should approach their cultural context: is it a battlefield or a mission field?[178]

Opposite the battling church, says Long, is the influencing church. The influencing church understands that at Pentecost "God created a new community through which God intends to reach people and redeem the world."[179] Elementary to this understanding is that God has given the church power through his Holy Spirit to accomplish the work of reaching all people with the gospel. Rather than seeing the church as a bastion of truth, the church becomes an outreach to people who have not accepted the gospel yet.

The influencing church is asking whether lasting cultural change comes through battling society or through influencing it. The battling church describes its enemies as "secular humanists, atheists with a hatred of God and religion and a well-defined and dangerous agenda."[180] Those in the influencing church see others as people created

---

[177] Long, 31.

[178] Op. Cit. 32.

[179] Tom Sine, *Cease Fire: Searching for Sanity in America's Culture Wars* (Grand Rapids, Michigan: Eerdmans 1995), 160.

[180] Pat Robertson, *Turning Tide*, (Dallas, Texas: Word, 1996), 151.

by God and in need of God, not as enemies of God. So their strategy is one of influence, dialogue, and a prophetic voice.[181]

The influencing church is motivated by the love of God for people and filled with hope that those people can in fact be reached because of God's power. Rather than being depressed about the demise of our world as we knew it, they are excited about the opportunities. Are the fields not ready to harvest (John 4:35)? Does the fact that Jesus has not returned yet not simply mean that there are yet people to whom the Father longs to be reconciled? – 2 Peter 3:9.

Motivated by the desire to see all people come to a saving knowledge of Jesus Christ, the influencing church designs and implements strategies that are effective for reaching the unchurched. They pray for the wisdom and guidance of the Holy Spirit. They ask the Father to use their efforts to draw all men to himself (John 12:32). And they believe the Scriptures, especially when Jesus promises his personal presence with them till the end of time.

Matthew 28:18-20

[18] And Jesus came up and spoke to them, saying, "All authority has been given to me in heaven and on earth. [19] Go therefore and make disciples of all the nations, baptizing them in the name of the Father and the Son and the Holy Spirit, [20] teaching them to observe all that I commanded you; and behold, I am with you always, even to the end of the age."

The church is Growing in Most Continents

Rather than being filled with dismay over the dismal state of our culture, world or denomination, we can rejoice that many positive things are happening in the world. Too often, we are ignorant of the fact that the church is growing

---

[181] Long, 32.

in most continents. Looking back to a time when Postmodernism was most virulent in its seminal influence there is reason to be hopeful.

According to David Barrett the percentage of practicing Christians as part of the global population jumped from 26.5% in 1970 to 30.7% in 1996. The percentage of "Great Commission Christians" as part of the global population jumped from 8.1% to 12.7% in the same time-period.[182]

Globalization is a good thing from the viewpoint of worldwide missions. Everywhere Christians are utilizing technology to be more efficient and strategic in reaching all people with the gospel. Christians are utilizing the internet in myriad ways. E-mail has provided a wonderful way for missionaries to have quick and relatively cheap contact with the home-front and for prayer requests to make their way around the world. The amount of computers in Christian use rose from 1000 in 1970 to 206,961,000 in 1996. In 1970 1,230 Christian radio and TV-stations reached 150,000,000 people. Twenty years later 3,200 stations were reaching 538,347,000 monthly listeners and viewers.[183]

Most exciting of all is the growth of the evangelical movement in South America. Walter Truett Anderson cites the following research: Richard Rodrigues reports that there are now more than 50 million Protestants in Latin America, that conversions are taking place at the rate of four hundred an hour and demographers are estimating that Latin America will be Evangelical by the end of the twenty-first century.[184] Together with the news of mass-movements

---

[182] David Barrett, "Status of Global Missions, 1996, in Context of the 20 and 21' Centuries" *International Bulletin of Missionary Research*, (January 1996), 21.

[183] Ibid ~ although I have grave doubts about the value of much that is presented by such T.V. and radio stations.

[184] Walter Truett Anderson, *Reality Isn't What It Used To Be*, (New York: Harper Collins Publishers, 1992), 204.

to saving faith come the reports of a massive missionary force coming to Europe and America from countries which themselves traditionally have been mission fields.

Chapter 5 The Postmodern Context

The hope of the Modern era was that scientific discovery and technological progress would bring an end to religion, the final triumph over superstition.[185] But nothing could have been further from the truth. While the modern expectation was that people would eventually abandon religion altogether on account of scientific progress, it would seem today that people are displaying a willingness to hold to one form of faith or another. Today an ever widening variety of religious movements enjoy a great deal of public interest. The situation causes Anderson to observe that we seem to be in a world with more religion than ever before.

> The situation is not necessarily heart-warming: the growth appears to have been quantitative rather than qualitative: there are more things to believe in, but not necessarily more of what we used to call belief. As G.K. Chesterton said, when people stop believing in God, the trouble is not that they believe in nothing, the trouble is that they will believe anything.[186]

Is the church engaging as effectively as it could in this new spiritual environment? Robert Nash doesn't think so:

> We play a little game each week in church called "Let's Pretend." We pretend that people want the same things from church in the 1990s that they wanted in the 1950s. We pretend the majority of Americans are church-going Christians who believe in the God of the Bible and who order their lives to reflect this reality. We pretend

---

[185] Walter Truett Anderson, *Reality Isn't What It Used To Be*, (New York: Harper Collins Publishers, 1992), 187.

[186] Ibid.

the spirituality of Americans in the 1990s is enhanced by a decades-old diet of practical faith, old-time religion, and personal "quiet time." We pretend that the church is still the center of community life and that people will come back to church "when they get their lives straightened out."[187]

The Postmodern era is confronting the church with a whole new culture, a new set of values and beliefs and practices. The question is, how will the church respond? Jimmy Long observes:

As the church stands today at this critical juncture, it needs to make sure it has enough information about these societal changes to make an informed decision. The church also needs to exercise enough faith to make a decision that might take it out of its current comfort zone. The decision that the church is making today about how it will relate to society will influence the church's mission for the next fifty to one hundred years.[188]

Understanding that we live in a society in which there are many alternatives to Christianity, Long recognizes that Generation X (which he terms the postmodern generation) if it is going to believe in Jesus Christ, will need to see that Christianity has something to offer that cannot be found in the culture at large.[189] In this process pop-culture can help us

---

[187] Robert N. Nash, Jr., *An 8-Track Church in a CD World* (Macon, Georgia: Smyth & Helwys Publishing, 1997), 2.

[188] Jimmy Long, *Generating Hope - A Strategy for Reaching the Postmodern Generation* (Downer's Grove, Illinois: InterVarsity Press, 1997), 18.

[189] Op. Cit., 21.

by being a resource for rethinking ministry as we seek to reach postmodern people.[190]

What We Encounter

If and when Christians realize their call and responsibility to reach this generation, and gear themselves into action, they will be confronted with people who are most probably quite different from themselves. Exactly what are they going to encounter? What are Postmodern people like?

Struggle with Doubt

Because Postmodern people are confronted with numerous lifestyles and worldviews alternative to their own every day, they regularly must deal with the challenges these pose to their own worldview and lifestyle. This distinguishes the Postmodern world from the world in which many older Christians grew up. In the modern world chances were that one would believe whatever one's parents and community believed. It was unlikely for a person to think twice about it; if one was not aware of worldviews other than one's own (and perhaps not even aware of having a worldview at all), chances are one would never question what one believed. Since people were seldom confronted with other worldviews, chances were they would never make a change in worldview, but hold to the same epistemology their entire life.[191]

The Postmodern era is vastly different. These days it takes a genuine effort to believe what one believes. "At the very least", writes James Hunter, "the binding address of faith…has weakened. Belief has not dissolved, but the

---

[190] Tom Beaudoin, *Virtual Faith*, (San Francisco: Jossey-Bass Publishers, 1998), 174.

[191] Even within multi-cultural societies in the Modern era religious communities were relatively segregated.

feeling of serene certainty has. Truth is no longer something unconsciously assumed, but something to which someone must consciously and intellectually assent."[192] Holding to a worldview can be a challenge, especially in the light of so many other conflicting ones.

Long quotes a student speaker at a Harvard graduation ceremony who summarized the feelings of many students of the time:

> I believe that there is one idea, one sentiment, which we have acquired at some point in our Harvard careers, and that ladies and gentlemen is in a word confusion... They tell us it is heresy to suggest the superiority of some value, fantasy to believe in moral argument, slavery to submit to a judgment sounder than your own. The freedom of our day is the freedom to devote ourselves to any values we please, on the mere condition that we do not believe them to be true.[193]

Living in this confusing world, postmodern people struggle with a sense of doubt or confusion. They must regularly deal with questions that challenge their own worldview, and the attraction offered by other worldviews. This brings a feeling of insecurity that affects both Christians and non-Christians.

It affects those who do not have a specific worldview to call their own. Since Postmodernism is incredulity towards all reigning thought structures, including the scientific worldview, how are we supposed to know what to believe? "Postmodernism," writes Scott Moore, "will aid us in helping people restore a healthy sense of doubt towards the mechanistic worldview, as it presents us with

---

[192] James D. Hunter, "What is Modernity? Historical roots and contemporary features", *Faith and Modernity*, eds. Philip Sampson, Vinay Samual, Chris Sugden (Oxford, United Kingdom: Regnum Books, 1994), 27.

[193] Robert Bellah, *The Good Society* (New York: Vintage, 1991), 43-44.

resources which can assist with the cultivation of this incredulity."[194] But if we cannot trust science anymore, and if such incredulity is cultivated in each of us, how can secular people ever believe in anything?

Doubt also affects Christians. In a world with many conflicting truth-claims, it is only natural that believers ask more questions of their own worldview, and at times have serious doubts about what they believe. The Christian faith in the twenty-first century has much competition, and consequently Christians are more likely to struggle with doubts. Questions about the truthfulness of our own beliefs, the degree of error in other beliefs, the eternal destination of those with other beliefs, the truthfulness of Scripture and others are likely to occupy the mind of a Christian in contemporary culture more regularly. Tom Beaudoin exemplifies the turmoil postmodern people can feel over such questions:

> I have attended worship services in various traditions, including Southern and American Baptist, reformed and conservative Jewish, Presbyterian, Lutheran, Episcopalian, Greek and Russian Orthodox, Messianic Jewish, Evangelical non-denominational, Pentecostal and Methodist. Although I do not fully agree with the teachings of any of these, I found the presence of God in each place of worship. Which one of these faiths is "true"? To say "all" of these sounds like dangerous relativism. To take an exclusivist position by responding "only my own" is not only condescending to the others but also does not square with my experience.[195]

---

[194] Scott H. Moore, "Era and Epoch, Epoch and Era: Christian Intellectuals in the Postmodern Turn," article published in *Christian Scholar's Review*, Volume XXVI, Number 2 (Winter 1996).

[195] Beaudoin, 121.

For some Christians who have grown up in a Christian home the confrontation with pluralism brings a crisis of faith. Why should they think they "hit the jackpot" just by being born in the right family? This was the experience of Robert Nash:

> I was haunted by a single thought: if Christianity is the only true religion, then how come Hindus and Muslims remain so committed to their particular faith traditions? Why can't they see the truth I see? This metropolitan environment created a faith crisis for me that the institutional church...now faces.[196]

Questions of doubt can in turn lead to a sense of guilt because doubt has traditionally been seen as a form of disbelief, compounding the problem.[197] They also contribute to a sense of insecurity that can surround us for a long time. Christian ministers will do well to cultivate strategies to help people deal with their doubt.

Intimately Fractured

Much has been written about the emotional brokenness of Generation X. While we can disagree over the question if families were healthier fifty or a hundred years ago, few would dispute that evident dysfunctionality among families is rampant today.

Different terms are used to describe exactly what is "wrong" with this generation of people. Barna, in *Christianity Today*, said they were the most "ignored, misunderstood, and disheartened generation our country has seen in a long time." In the same article Richard Price,

---

[196] Nash, 28-29.

[197] See Os Guinness, *Doubt: Faith in Two Minds*, (Lion, 2nd Rev. Ed., 1983) for a very helpful treatment of Doubt.

professor of evangelism at Fuller Theological Seminary, calls this "a clinically depressed generation."[198]

In his book, *Reinventing Your Church*, Brian McLaren argues that a new era demands a new church. That church will have to deal with people who are "rawer" raw material then churches have experienced so far. By this, he means that the trajectory they have to travel in order to become mature disciples of Jesus Christ is longer. We must start with people in all their "rawness" and offer them the hope of becoming, as new Christians, agents of the new church in the new world on the other side.[199]

What is meant by "intimately fractured"? In the areas of their life where human beings are designed to experience intimacy, X'ers are fractured. They have many pieces, but the puzzle does not fit together anymore. Social changes, changes in paradigm, and the high degree to which family life has become dysfunctional have all contributed to this situation.

The problem is widespread and severe. Author William Mahedy had worked with Vietnam veterans for a long time before he started counseling Generation X'ers. The condition he and many other therapists found among veterans was termed, "Post-Traumatic Stress Disorder" (PTSD). PTSD is an enduring condition that results from a very stressful incident beyond the normal range of human experiences (combat, terrorism, genocide, torture, rape, violence, devastating natural disasters).

> When a person is threatened with physical harm or psychic disintegration, the only business at hand is survival. Disastrous events generate their own overpowering emotional responses: sorrow,

---

[198] Cited by Tapia, Ibid.

[199] Brian McLaren, *Reinventing your Church* (Grand Rapids, Michigan: Zondervan, 1998), 33.

grief, guilt, anger. These emotions are entirely appropriate, but to allow them to surface during the crisis would be dangerous to life, well-being and sanity. The only option is to bury them deeply.

Yet repressed emotions of this intensity always resurface in one form or another and always cause trouble. Dreams, flashbacks, sleep disorders, violent behavior, depression, emotional numbing, feelings of detachment from others and inability to have loving feelings are some of the symptoms. An inability to feel emotion (called psychic numbing) is a root symptom of PTSD.[200]

When Mahedy started working with a campus ministry, he was shocked to find how many young people suffered from PTSD. He says PTSD is now widespread among X'ers, and many other disorders, such as Borderline Personality Disorder and Identity Disorder, also seem very prevalent.[201]

Countless young people were psychologically or sexually abused as children, and a great many young women have been raped. Growing numbers of youth are exposed to gang violence and random drive-by shootings in our cities. These young people are in a real war zone. Many of them suffer from clinical PTSD and may require therapy.[202]

As a result of the traumatic experiences they have grown up with, X'ers typically carry a lot of emotional baggage. Besides anger, rage, grief and emotional

---

[200] William Mahedy and Janet Bernardi, *A Generation Alone - X'ers Making a Place in the World* (Downer Grove, Illinois, IVP Press, 1994), 25-26.

[201] Op. Cit., 28, 79

[202] Op. Cit. 26 ff.

brokenness, they also have a strong sense of guilt and shame. Many Postmodern people have a keen sense of guilt and shame which results from their own behavior. Often they also struggle with such feelings because they blame themselves somehow for the experiences that have scarred them while they were young. Long makes a helpful distinction between guilt and shame, explaining that in contemporary culture this distinction has been lost.

> Because the baby-boom generation grew up primarily under the influence of the Enlightenment, it tends to be guilt based. Generation X, having grown up mainly under the influence of postmodernism, can be characterized as shame based. X'ers feel bad not so much for what they have or have not done but about who they are. Guilt is based on the violation of an objective standard. Guilt says *I have done something wrong*. Guilt can be absolved when the penalty for the wrong has been satisfied. Then the perpetrator of the wrongful act can be pardoned for the wrong and forgiven for the act. Shame says, *There is something wrong with me*. Shame has less to do with actions, and more to do with a loss of identity and being. Shame cannot be removed as easily as guilt. It is easier for us to change our actions than to change our very being. Shame is the primary cause of emotional distress in our time. It is a byproduct of the social changes and the dysfunctional families of our day.[203]

The confrontation with so much personal brokenness can sometimes be disheartening. The good news is that Postmodern people are generally well aware of their

---

[203] Long, 163. It is perhaps difficult to see shame in a culture that so flaunts its depravity at times. Yet most counselors and therapists are adamant that this distinction between shame and guilt is very important for counselors dealing with intimately fractured people.

brokenness, and have an intuitive need for God. Their brokenness moves them away from the pride of self-sufficiency that so often marked their Modern predecessors, and can create in people a sense that they need God. Douglas Coupland displays that attitude very well:

Now here is my secret:

I tell it to you with an openness of heart that I doubt I shall ever achieve again, so I pray that you are in a quiet room as you hear these words. My secret is that I need God -- that I am sick and can no longer make it alone. I need God to help me give, because I no longer seem to be capable of giving; to help me be kind, as I no longer seem capable of kindness; to help me love, as I seem beyond being able to love.[204]

The need for relationship is probably the biggest need Postmodern people have. Abandoned, broken and violated, they are desperately looking for a relationship that will last. As Tom Beaudoin writes:

That is why I boil down the religious quest of Gen X pop culture to one question that begins on the most intimate level possible and in the midst of profound ambiguity. Our most fundamental question is "Will you be there for me?" We ask this of ourselves, bodies, parents, friends, partners, society, religions, leaders, nation, and even God. The frailty that we perceive threatening all of these relationships continually provokes us to ask this question.[205]

---

[204] Douglas Coupland, *Life After God* (New York: Pocket Books, 1994) 359. It is interesting that this quote comes from Coupland, who is also the author 'Generation X', the novel that made the term so popular as a label.

[205] Beaudoin, 140. Beaudoin goes on to contrast this quest for relationship with the central question of the Boomer-generation, which he defines as: "What is the meaning of my life?"

Fluidity of Personality and Worldview

A result of the personal brokenness of X'ers, is that their personalities have lost their solidity and become fluid. Not only does it take X'ers longer to develop a healthy sense of who they are, they actually refuse to lock themselves into a particular personal identity, because to do so would not be advantageous.

An obvious example of the influence of Postmodernism is that people now defend the idea that who they are depends on the context they are in, not on who they were divinely created or biologically determined to be. Robert Jay Lifton argues that what we are seeing is the emergence of a new kind of person, which he terms the Protean man.

> Now we know from Greek mythology that Proteus was able to change his shape with relative ease from wild boar to lion to dragon to fire to flood. What he found difficult, and would not do unless seized and chained, was to commit himself to a single form, a form most his own, and carry out his function of prophecy. We can say the same of Protean man, but we must keep in mind his possibilities as well as difficulties. The protean style of self-process, then, is characterized by an interminable series of experiments and explorations, some shallow, some profound, each of which can be readily abandoned in favor of still new, psychological quests.[206]

Lifton goes on to say that this pattern of behavior resembles "identity diffusion or confusion," in which impaired psychological functioning can be present, but doesn't necessarily need to be. To grasp this "style", as he

---

[206] Robert Jay Lifton, "The Protean Style", in *The Truth About the Truth*, ed. Walter Truett Anderson (New York: Tacker Putnam Books, 1995), 130. This is what Gergen calls multiphrenia. See Kenneth J. Gergen, *The Saturated Self* (New York: Basic Books, 1991).

terms it, we must alter our judgments concerning what is psychologically disturbed or pathological, as opposed to what is adaptive or even innovative.[207]

We see this fluidity in personality in the ability of X'ers to be like chameleons who adjust their personality, character and appearance to every situation. But this ability to be "all things to all men" is purely pragmatic and self-serving: to get the most out of every situation. They have been well-educated by the millions of commercials they have been bombarded with. They sell themselves well.

This fluidity can express itself on many levels. X'ers will change their fashion-style depending on the situation and the people they are with. They will change their taste, their preferences if they need to. They will shift between groups of friends, assuming different roles and personalities in each, and feel surprisingly little discomfort by this apparent lack of authenticity. This is interesting, because, while Protean man does not expect much authenticity within himself/herself, s/he does seek it in others. In certain situations he/she is willing to change sexual preference, perhaps even gender. And they will change ideas, political ideologies and personal worldviews as the need demands.

Their willingness to change worldviews will impact the way Christians perceive them as a "target audience" in evangelistic efforts. Lifton writes:

> Thus political and religious movements, as they confront Protean man, are likely to have much less difficulty convincing him to alter previous convictions than they do providing them with a set of beliefs which can demand his allegiance for more than a brief experimental interlude.[208]

---

[207] Op. Cit. 131.

[208] Op. Cit. 132.

Anderson refers to this attitude towards worldviews and religions as "ready to wear religion."[209] People wear their religion as a coat, which keeps them warm when it is cold and dry when it is raining. But they are equally willing to shed the coat when the sun comes out or retire the old coat in exchange for a new one if a new fashion or gimmick comes along.[210]

This fluidity in personality does, however, have a price-tag: confusion about who I really am is the obvious result. Writes Tom Beaudoin, "X'ers have a sense of self that, in its fragmentation, simulates the real, undivided self that we were assumed to have. We simulate unity by calling ourselves "I" even though we are sometimes unsure of which self "I" represents."[211]

A Need for Hope

In the midst of all the challenges that Postmodern people face, what they lack is hope. To Postmodern people nothing is certain anymore, ethics has become purely personal and happiness seems to be within reach only for some and elusive for most. Perhaps even more influential is the fact that X'ers are well acquainted with the breakdown of relationships, and consequently have little confidence in the endurability of a relationship with anybody. And yet it is their biggest need.

Under these conditions a constant feeling of despair has become commonplace. "Most of us in the postmodern world," writes Jimmy Long, "are changing from belief in progress (future hope) to resignation in the face of human misery (present despair)."[212] At the same time, writes

---

[209] Anderson, *Reality Isn't What it Used to Be*, 187-227.

[210] For this analogy also see Nash, 7.

[211] Beaudoin, 140.

[212] Long, 115.

Andres Tapia, this generation lacks even the memory of a hope-giving gospel.[213]

A Rejection of Dogmatism and a Desire for Experience

Postmodern people are further distinguished from Modern people in that they tend to prioritize experience over rational content. This can put them at odds with many evangelical churches, where the emphasis is on "the right content of our faith" as opposed to "do we experience what we believe?" I think this is one contributing factor to the increase in popularity of Pentecostal and Charismatic churches ~ people tend to gravitate to these instead of the more "theological" churches where the predominant emphasis is on the Word and tend to be perceived as too cerebral, almost like a theological seminary.

This situation causes Stanley Grenz to say: "where the church in the modern era attempted, with varying degrees of success, to lead people to a realization of the truth through a rationalistic, cognitive process, the church in the postmodern era must become post-rationalistic."[214] Is it possible that we have in fact erred in giving too much attention to the rational aspects of our faith? If so, then perhaps our confrontation with Postmodernism can help us restore balance. Real faith is not a matter of just knowing the correct body of truth. It is an act of the whole person. This includes the use of reason but is not merely restricted to only that.

If Modernism put too much emphasis on the reasonability of faith, it may well be that Postmodernism puts too much emphasis on experience. Be that as it may,

---

[213] Tapia, 18.

[214] Stanley J. Grenz, *Primer on Postmodernism* (Grand Rapids, Michigan: Eerdmans, 1996), 169.

the Modern era has left a vacuum behind in which people are crave experience. In this new context, people want to experience what we preach before they put their lives on the line. Jimmy Long states that for Postmodern people truth is not so much stated as it is experienced.[215] Tom Beaudoin agrees: "Gen X pop culture exhibits an experimental attitude toward orthodoxy."[216] And so does Robert Nash:

> As the culture has become increasingly interested in spirituality, the church has become highly rational and propositional in its approach to faith. It has defined spirituality as that body of truth that must be believed. Spirituality has been reduced to the rote memorization of Scripture and the defense of propositional truths about God. God is to be obeyed, not experienced.[217]

This state of affairs causes Robert Nash to argue that the church must quit shoring up propositional truth about God while ignoring the need for an experience with God.[218] The need for experience is genuine, not just a thrill-seeking endeavor. Postmodern people realize all too well that just about anything can be proven to be true by rational arguments, or conversely false, by the same. There are too many heavily defended viewpoints and beliefs in this world to trust in any one of them based solely on arguments. Confronted with an explosion of knowledge Postmodern people do not trust their own reasoning abilities anymore because they understand them to be inadequate. They would rather put their confidence in something that is real, and can be verified to be so by ways of experience.

---

[215] Long, 45.

[216] Beaudoin, 125.

[217] Nash, 3.

[218] Op. Cit., 62.

Suspicion and Rejection of Organized, Institutionalized Religion

Tom Beaudoin lists this as the first of four main themes in the approach of Generation X to religion. It is not a rejection of faith, or even of religion itself. On the contrary, says Beaudoin, Generation X is deeply religious in many ways. But there is a very fundamental distrust of organized and institutional religion. One could say that X'ers are being spiritual without needing institutional religion.

What causes such severe distrust? First, there is a basic distrust of institutions in general which is not aimed at churches or Christianity specifically. Institutions are viewed as bureaucracies in which care and attention for the individual get lost. Typically, institutions consist of enormous hierarchies, where decisions are made at the top at the expense of those at the bottom. Consequently, X'ers have a disregard for hierarchies.[219] Second, the distrust arises as a result of the frequency with which large institutions (religious or otherwise) make the news because they are being investigated for corruption, dodging the law, or malpractice. Regretfully corruption of one kind or another has not left the church untainted. In the media the immoral escapades of well-known televangelists make headline news. In the newspapers we frequently read of the sexual misconduct of clergy and many are aware of situations where power and money were misused for one purpose or another. X'ers are all too aware of this. Andres Tapia writes, "Having grown up amidst headlines about fallen televangelists and crooked politicians, X'er trust in authority figures is low, and cynicism of anything organized, like the church and political parties, is high.[220]

---

[219] Lawrence I. Bradford and Claire Raines, *Twenty Something - Managing & Motivating Today's New Work Force* (Denver, Colorado: Merrill-Alexander Publishing, 1992), 37.

[220] Tapia, 19.

Beaudoin lists three ways this culture of suspicion of organized religion expresses itself. "First X'ers challenge religious institutions in general. Second, Gen X'ers specifically assault the Catholic Church. Third, they frequently pit Jesus against the Church."[221] The reason for this last form of rebellion against the church is that X'ers perceive a dichotomy between Jesus and the church. X'ers have two objections against the church.

First, their perception is that there are so many churches out there, all claiming to be the true way while speaking critically of other churches. As X'ers do not understand the theological differences that separate these churches, this variety of churches is in fact confusing them. While their understanding of Jesus is perhaps limited, X'ers are often very sure about one thing: this is not what Jesus had in mind.

Secondly, they perceive the church as having become extremely institutionalized. The vitality and joy X'ers are looking for seems to have disappeared. Instead, these "atrophied ministries often encourage boredom, indifference, or outright rebellion on the part of the faithful."[222] Whatever the problem, X'ers don't quite feel they are likely to encounter Jesus at church. Instead, they wonder why the church matters, and even wonder if the church matters to God.[223]

Craving Community

It is unfortunate that Postmodern people feel they have so much reason to dislike the church, because they do have

---

[221] Beaudoin, 41.

[222] Op. Cit., 51.

[223] Ibid. Of course God loves the church (Ephesians 5:25b-27), though not necessarily all its institutionalized forms.

a tremendous craving for community.[224] Having observed institutions at work Postmodern people realize that the uniqueness and the individuality of an individual quickly get lost in the machinery of these institutions. Churches are no exception to the rule. And yet X'ers are hungry for relationship, a place to belong.

This desire for community, which is very strong, is caused by several factors. It stems from the Postmodern culture in which we live. The desire to belong to an "identity-giving group" has given rise to what sociologists call the "New Tribalism." As we saw in chapter 2, the group or tribe one is part of, has a grand story, a "meta-narrative", that conveys the worldview of that group, which in turn determines the meaning of life, values, and morals of that group. Without such a group or community to be part of, the individual is utterly lost in an existence without meaning and direction.[225]

The desire for community is also a result of all the broken relationships X'ers experience. Jimmy Long writes:

> It is hard for young people, especially, to develop a sense of connection when their families have little if any stability. As Veith says, "Whereas traditional communities (families, villages, churches) gave a sense of belonging and permanence, the contemporary social scene is characterized by impermanence."[226] With the breakdown of the family and the loss of any national consensus, we are becoming a culture of

---

[224] Long, 50, 70, 134-210. The desire for community is the single-most identified need of Generation X by authors on the subject.

[225] Op. Cit., 70-71. See also Grenz, 63; Carson, 15.

[226] Gene Edward Veith, Jr., *Postmodern Times - A Christian Guide to Contemporary Thought and Culture* (Wheaton, Illinois: Crossway Books, 1994), 86.

homeless people who search continually for a place to belong.[227]

The desire and need for community also stem from what some call the constant state of aloneness that many Postmodern people share. Aloneness, writes Long, is different from Loneliness.

> Loneliness is a state of emptiness, whereas aloneness can occur amid a plethora of activities, even dance music. Aloneness causes and is caused by a distrust of people that stems from a fear of being hurt one more time. At the root of it is a fear of being neglected or abandoned that leads to alienation from people, sometimes even one's closest friends. While aloneness is a survival technique, it can come across as independence. Essentially, aloneness is a state of the soul.[228]

Mahedy and Bernardi concur:

> Aloneness is the enduring result of abandonment. It is the spiritual residence of those who have been abandoned. Aloneness goes beyond even the deprivation of citizenship in a community; that is implied by the word *alienation*. In aloneness, one's life is filled with nothing but the clutter and busyness and, all too often, the painful memories one's own past.[229]

Aloneness can become the crossroads from which people start looking for others, and for God. It can send people looking for the community they so desperately need and desire. For such aloneness there is also only one cure: it

---

[227] Long, 72.

[228] Op. Cit., 49.

[229] Mahedy and Bernardi, 32.

can only be cured by being part of a community ~ ultimately the community of God.[230]

Openness to the Supernatural

With the demise of Modernism with its reliance on the rational part of human being, there is hunger to explore the spiritual realities that are part of life. Through media and travel, Westerners have come in contact with the fact that other cultures experience spiritual realities, and they evaluate the lack of experience of such realities as a form of poverty within their own culture.

At the same time, it is becoming increasingly apparent that rationalism and empiricism are imperfect ways to "knowing". Disenchanted with the pursuit of rationalism and its yield Postmodern people are desperately seeking the spiritual, where new avenues need to be explored. "I am fascinated by the spiritual man; I am humbled by his humble nature" sang Alanis Morissette.[231]

While Postmodern people tend to reject organized religion for a wide variety of reasons, this does not mean they have all become atheists and agnostics. On the contrary, several cultural observers have commented on "a revival of spirituality," which finds expression in fashion, music, art, movies, etc.[232] Tom Beaudoin says:

> I began to notice how the popular culture seemed suffused with religious references. Our popular songs, music videos, and movies were about sin, salvation, and redemption, among

---

[230] Unfortunately churches have often failed to be that community. Nash laments that the church has failed to reflect the kind of community that will exist in the kingdom of God. Nash, 3.

[231] Alanis Morisette, "All I Really Want." From the album *Jagged Little Pill* (MCA Music Publishing, 1995).

[232] See e.g. Nash, 49.

other themes. Contrary to common perception, we appeared to have a very theological culture. Perhaps we were even a religious generation.[233]

The religiosity of Generation X, as Tom Beaudoin describes it, however, is not for the sake of the pursuit of truth, or even for the sake of correspondence to reality. Their argument goes that whatever we believe does not need to necessarily match the truth out there (if there is such a thing in the first place). If there is a pursuit in it, it is that of personal fulfillment. Who cares if it is real, as long as it makes you feel better.

This creates a dichotomy: the practice associated with faith is deemed more important than the content of the faith...

> Modern day spirituality is often associated with the desire for the mystical. In a doctrinal religion the initiate or convert is presented with a clearly visible body of information to learn. Study your catechism, kid. In a mystical tradition the student is given to understand that the truth is not learned in that fashion; the truth is something one must discover for oneself. The history of religion is a history of the two tendencies pushing and pulling at one another.[234]

If that were true, then it would seem that currently history is moving in the direction of a search for the mystical, after a period of approaching matters of faith very intellectually. After having approached the transcendent with a sense of pride, thinking we could understand it, we are now moving back (or forward) to desiring an experience of the transcendent.

---

[233] Beaudoin, 14.

[234] Anderson, 213.

The interest in spiritual matters and mysticism expresses itself in many ways. In an article in *Time*, Tamala Edwards described an escalating interest in Monastic life:

> Across the country, Catholic monasteries and convents, usually regarded as strange or the stuff of medieval myth, are besieged with would-be retreatants and booked months in advance...While organized church retreats are not new, what is startling is that much of the increase is in individual retreatants, including many Protestants and even non-Christians.[235]

This desire for transcendence affects Christians and non-Christians alike. Commenting on a growing enchantment with the worship styles of other traditions by evangelicals, Gary Burge quoted one of his students in an article in *Christianity Today*, entitled: "Are Evangelicals Missing God at Church?"

> I think that much of modern society has lost a sense of divine, holy space. This became obvious to me in our church architecture. Gymnasiums and impermanent buildings have replaced the splendor and holiness of cathedrals, which created the ultimate feeling of divine space. A sanctuary should be a place that is completely separate - that radiates the holiness of God. Plastic cups and folding chairs are not enough. There has to be an environment that communicates God's holiness to my senses and to my spirit.[236]

---

[235] Tamala Edwards, "Get Thee to a Monastery", TIME (U.S. edition) August 3, 1998, 52.

[236] Gary M. Burge, "Are Evangelicals Missing God at Church?" *Christianity Today*, 6 October 1997, 22. One does not necessarily have to agree with this opinion but it is interesting that a young person at the end of the twentieth-century expressed it.

A Desire for Stories

Postmodern people understand that truths and beliefs are better communicated through stories than through propositions. Reducing truth to propositions filters out the background, the details which may be so necessary for understanding in the first place. Not just what is said matters, but also how it is said. This is because:

> Story is a primary language of experience. Telling and listening to a story has the same structure as our experience...The episodes of our lives take place one after another just like a story. One of the ways we know each other is by telling stories. We live in stories.[237]

At the same time, postmodern people have experienced a breakdown of confidence in rationalism. They no longer believe that morality can be derived from reason instead of religion. They no longer believe that knowledge is inherently good.[238] This means that an apologetic that is heavy on rationality will not enjoy nearly as much success in the Postmodern era as it did in the Modern era. Postmodern people simply will not be led to Christ through a process of logical deduction and theological propositions on a large scale: "nobody believes in God because of rational argumentation anyway."[239] The Postmodern context is going to demand a new apologetic, one that focuses on stories more than propositions.

---

[237] Thomas E. Boornershine, *Story Journey - an Invitation to the Gospel as Storytelling* (Nashville: Abingdon, 1985), 18.

[238] Leighton G. Ford and Jim Denney, *The Power of Story - Rediscovering the Oldest, most Natural Way to Reach People for Christ* (Colorado Springs, CO: NavPress, 1994), 37-39.

[239] Arthur Schafer, "Does God Exist?" A debate hosted by Campus Crusade at the University of Manitoba, Winnipeg, Jan. 19, 1998.

A Desire for Holism

With the rise of the New Age movement the word holism has generally had bad connotations for many Christians. But for Postmodern people, holism is a central principle to their epistemology: truth, whatever that may be, cannot be simplistic, reductionist and narrow. It must of necessity pertain to the body, mind, and soul, as opposed to the Modernist emphasis and preference for the mind over the others. The Postmodern desire for holism is a critique of the dualism that was central to Modernism. In the pursuit for reason-unswayed-by-passion, this dualism split mind and body, reason and passions. Such dualism is replaced by the postmodern understanding that passion and reason are inextricably interwoven.[240]

A Strong Conviction that Oppression of Any Kind Is Wrong

Because of all the information we have at our fingertips, through education, the media and the internet, we are confronted daily with the fact that millions of people do not enjoy the freedom that is so dear to us in the West. Not only do people far away experience oppression, but closer to home it seems that many people-groups protest that they experience oppression as well. Battle-lines are drawn between those who oppose abortion and those who advocate it as a woman's right to choose. Bitter arguments fly between those who favor school prayer and those who do not. Between those wanting to save the rain forest and those needing rain forest trees to keep their businesses going, it looks like every group either feels

---

[240] Dan R Stiver, "The Uneasy Alliance between Evangelicalism and Postmodernism: A Reply to Anthony Thiselton," in *The Challenge of Postmodernism - An Evangelical Engagement*, ed., David S. Dockery (Wheaton, Illinois: BridgePoint, 1995), 244-5.

116

oppressed, or is accused of being oppressive, or a little of both.

Postmodern people wonder "can't we all just get along?" "In a world where everyone lives according to differing theories, it is far better to practice tolerance and appreciate diversity than to capsize the boat by stirring up controversy."[241] But while Postmodernism is tolerant of all and everything, it is intolerant of those it perceives to be intolerant. Because Christianity has historically been associated with intolerance on various occasions, Postmodern people now regard Christianity with a suspicious eye, if not an outright conviction that Christianity is by definition intolerant.[242]

People with a Postmodern mindset are convinced that notions of absolute truth and their exclusive claims are intolerant and oppressive. The Postmodern answer to this is simple. All faiths need to be put back in their proper place. You can believe what you want to, as long as you realize that what you believe is in fact only that; a belief.

It seems many Christians feel threatened by this notion. That is understandable, for the Christian faith does purport to be true ~ not just for some, but for all. Christians are quick to point out that the surrounding culture is becoming intolerant of Christian beliefs and practices in many ways.

It is easy to forget that evangelicals share a strong agreement with Postmodernists, in that they, too, believe that oppression is wrong. As Christians living in the Postmodern world we need to wonder if our cause and Lord are served by our desire to protect ourselves by accusing the surrounding culture of intolerance towards us. Shouldn't we rather join the fight against oppression? The

---

[241] McLaren, 88.

[242] For an excellent analysis of the concept of "tolerance" as used by today's culture, see Carson, 32-37.

Postmodern context demands that we make every effort that we can to carry out the message of the gospel in a way that respects and uplifts the other. The message of the gospel is that Jesus came to set us free from the oppression of sin and death, the ultimate of all oppression. The gospel is explicit both in its rejection of the strife for personal power and status, and its affirmation of service and love as the right approach to the surrounding world.[243]

Following Christ in the Postmodern era also means suffering with and for others.[244] First of all, there is a perception that global happiness is not around the corner, and that suffering is part of life. Second, the image of Christians suffering for their faith may be the strongest antidote to the impression that Christianity is a faith of violence and oppression. As we seek to reach postmodern people with the gospel the obvious question then is: how can churches reach Postmodern people?

---

[243] Anthony C. Thiselton, *Interpreting God and the Postmodern Self*, (Grand Rapids Michigan: Eerdmans, 1995), 19.

[244] Alan Padgett, "Christianity and Postmodernity," article published in *Christian Scholar's Review*, Volume XXVI, Number 2 (Winter 1996), Special Issue: Christianity and PostModernity.

CHAPTER 6 Values for Postmodern Ministry

Having studied the Postmodern worldview in chapter 3, and the Postmodern context in chapter 5, we are now ready to investigate the more practical avenues open to us in reaching Postmodern people. In this chapter we will look at some of the general values that should characterize our ministry.

Humility

Contempt for institutions is a bedrock component of X'er spirituality, as Tom Beaudoin states, it is of fundamental importance that we return to humility in ministry.[245] Since X'ers have such an astute understanding of institutions' limited and tentative nature, it would benefit religious organizations to seek to understand X'er criticisms. Popular culture challenges the church to preach and practice from a place of weakness and humility.[246]

We need humility in three ways. First, we need humility in the way we handle the truth. Robert Nash says the church must learn to ask questions, instead of constantly spouting answers. By asking questions, Christians exhibit humility, a trait the church rarely expressed when its spiritual domination was unchallenged. Perhaps that is why the fairgoers [people living in the postmodern world] today have so much trouble accepting the essential truths of Christianity.[247] Nash writes:

---

[245] Tom Beaudoin, *Virtual Faith*, (San Francisco: Jossey-Bass Publishers, 1998), 161.

[246] Ibid.

[247] Robert N. Nash, Jr., *An 8-Track Church in a CD World* (Macon, Georgia: Smyth & Helwys Publishing, 1997), 38.

I believe in the Christian story. I believe with all my heart that Jesus Christ is Emmanuel - God with us - and that Christ suffered with humanity in his death and overcame death through resurrection. The sin of my broken relationship with God and other human beings is forgiven through Jesus Christ. But I also recognize that these are simply faith assertions. I have no proof of these truths except the proof I know within my own heart. And I cannot become overconfident that this truth will win the world over simply because I believe it to be the only Truth.[248]

Second, we need to acknowledge that we do not know the whole truth. While we may believe the Bible to be divine revelation, and therefore true from cover to cover, it does not answer every question that we can ask in our curiosity. We must acknowledge that there are in fact many areas of life where the Bible is silent. It tells us little, if anything, about physiology, quantum mechanics and astronomy. Insights from these and other fields can, in fact, help us in our understanding of life and the universe. There is no place for an attitude of "we are the people of the book, and we have the answers to everything" and it is unfortunate that such an attitude of superiority has in the past hurt the testimony of the gospel. Lesslie Newbigin points out that, "It is essential to the integrity of our witness that we recognize that to be its witnesses does not mean to be possessors of all truth."[249]

Third, we must recognize the true nature of the truth that we know. While we have sought to defend our faith as being reasonable, perhaps even logical, and maybe even obvious, we have ignored the fact that the very nature of

---

[248] Op. Cit., 34.

[249] Lesslie Newbigin, The Gospel in a Pluralist Society, (Grand Rapids, Michigan: Eerdmans Publishing Company, 1989), 12.

the gospel is foolishness to the world. How can the gospel ever seem reasonable to the world, if by its very nature, it goes against everything the world stands for?[250]

We've spent centuries trying to explain the reasons behind Christ's death on the cross. When we're perfectly honest, none of our high and lofty explanations make any sense whatsoever. Some Christians have framed elaborate defenses of the resurrection. Other who profess to be Christians have explained the resurrection away by insisting that belief in it is not an essential faith requirement. None of our explanations have entirely satisfied anyone. So, in the end, we're left with nonsense. Not a single doctrine or story of belief makes any sense. We will never prove any of it. The only place to start is with the foolishness of it all. I believe it. You believe it. Other people believe it. We believe that God became flesh and dwelt among us. And the power of it rests on that belief. It does not rest on any justification that I can make of it. And no scientific proof can make it more believable to me than that.[251]

To put it in Postmodern terms, we must recognize that we have a story. In addition, while we believe in the truthfulness of that story with all our hearts, we have no means to prove that story as true. Our only hope can be that as we share our story boldly, much like the apostles in

---

[250] Lesslie Newbigin argues that in defending the reasonableness of the gospel we have actually accommodated to the Modern worldview and violated the nature of the gospel. "The defense is in fact a tactical retreat" Op. Cit., 3. Newbigin is perceived as a controversial figure by some evangelicals because of his partnership in the World Council of Churches, and his unwillingness to commit to a more evangelical view of the Bible. But having ministered in India for 36 years, and many years in England after that, he is considered somewhat of an expert when it comes to ministry in pluralistic society.

[251] Nash, 45.

the book of Acts, people will find faith in their hearts as the Holy Spirit moves them.

Sensitivity

The Postmodern context demands that we do our evangelism with sensitivity. We should be mindful of the fact that people's knowledge of the role of Christians in history makes them extra sensitive to what they feel is our intolerance towards them and those of other convictions or lifestyles.[252] An in-your-face proclamation of "this is the truth, and you will go to hell if you don't believe it" is unlikely to be helpful in bringing people to Christ. This is because their beliefs are the result of personal preference and not solid external foundation. An attack on their personal beliefs will be perceived as a personal attack. Everyone has the right to his or her own opinion. They do not mind if you do not agree with them, but they will become defensive if you try to change their opinions.[253] This is not to say we cannot be bold, for indeed we must tell our story with boldness. However, as we discuss the values of successful ministry to Postmoderns, it is imperative that we realize that being bold is not the same as being offensive. Postmodern people are all too aware of Christian shortcomings, and it will be very easy for us to perpetuate negative impressions people have of us. However, if we could analyze what would win people, or how we could approach them in a way they are not expecting, then perhaps we have a chance of sharing our faith.

---

[252] Alan Padgett, "Christianity and Postmodernity," article published in *Christian Scholar's Review*, Volume)0(VI, Number 2 (Winter 1996), Special Issue: Christianity and PostModernity.

[253] Gene Edward Veith, Jr., *Postmodern Times - A Christian Guide to Contemporary Thought and Culture* (Wheaton, Illinois: Crossway Books, 1994), 176.

Authenticity and Honesty

The Postmodern age has in part been formed by examples of "fallen leadership" ~ leaders who have fallen prey to sexual temptation, corruption, coercion, power ploys and political intrigue. Dubious behavior comes as no surprise to Postmodern people ~ we know that we all struggle in similar ways. The double lives of pastors, princes, and presidents have simply been too well documented for postmodern people to believe, even for one moment, in the absence of personal moral struggles in the lives of leaders.

> Relationships between men and women, parents and children, no longer seemed transparent but were perceived to conceal dark secrets and self-deceptions. When stories of private life (once thought separate from the public sphere) became the stuff of everyday publishing, innocence became implausible.[254]

When leaders portray themselves as morally strong and successful, especially in matters of character, they become unbelievable to Postmodern people. In the Modern age leadership was characterized by being strong and achieving; in the Postmodern age the leader who portrays himself as "a fellow-struggler" will find a hearing sooner. People will find it easier to identify with a fellow-struggler because they are all too well acquainted with their own brokenness and inability to do good.[255]

Postmodern people understand authenticity in another way too. To them, authenticity is not only "doing what

---

[254] Dave Fitzgerald, "The Future of Belief," *First Things*, 63 May 1996, 23-27.

[255] An illustration of this is the readiness of the American public to forgive President Clinton after his confession in the Lewinsky-affair, and their desire for him to "get on with the job."

you say." It also means that you do not pretend to have a coherent and all-inclusive system of truth. It is considered authentic to admit that "you cannot fit all the puzzle pieces together." Conversely, not to admit your inability to do so is perceived as inauthentic. We should be aware of this understanding of authenticity, and the culture's search for it.

A Holistic Approach

The Postmodern worldview rejects the Modern dualism that separates mind over heart and elevates the former over the latter. Educated to think systematically, they view the world as consisting of systems and their sub-parts. Postmodern people know intuitively that reality is complex, and they will, therefore, reject any approach that is simplistic or reductionist which leaves no place for wonder and mystery. And they will certainly reject any evangelistic appeal that rests solely on rational arguments. How could they accept the claims of a gospel that purports to affect the whole human being, but, in essence, has to be accepted on rational grounds alone? If this gospel indeed is good for the whole being, then postmodern people will want to experience it before they commit heart and soul. Jimmy Long says, "In a Postmodern world where logic and reasoning are not a given and where the emotions are more in evidence, an approach to discipleship that emphasizes only reason will fail miserably."[256]

How can Postmodern people experience the truth of what we believe, if they themselves do not believe it? There are a number of ways. Here are some examples. They can observe and enjoy our community. If indeed we are able to foster a healthy sense of community, Scripture tells us this will demonstrate the love of God to them (John 17:21-23). They can also enjoy our worship. While they

---

[256] Long, 162.

may not understand everything, and, in fact, find some things strange, the presence of God can sometimes be very tangible in worship, even to unbelievers. Lastly, they can enjoy the benefits of prayer as we go to the Father on their behalf.[257]

This new context should be receptive to the gospel. The gospel affects more than just the mind; "it penetrates even to dividing soul and spirit, joints and marrow; it judges the thoughts and attitudes of the heart" (Hebrews 4:12). Where Modernism "directed us to give precedence to narrow specializations of knowledge, postmodernists seek the wisdom that promotes human wholeness."[258] The gospel is that wholeness, and it provides an answer, or, at least, the direction of where that answer can be found, for every epistemological question.

Clear Ethics

Evangelicals frequently bemoan the ever-continuing landslide in morals and ethics they perceive all around them. The loss of faith in anything, coupled with the continual pursuit of personal happiness, make for a climate in which anything goes, and nothing is wrong. Having grown up in that climate, Postmodern people are left with a need for moral direction.

As Christians, we must understand that "our story" is logically before our morals. The story, says Leighton Ford,

---

[257] The Kingdom of Heaven, as Jesus presented it, was very much a demonstrative Kingdom. Perhaps this is somewhat of a return to that?

[258] John A. Sims, "Postmodernism: The Apologetic Imperative" in *The Challenge of Postmodernism - An Evangelical Engagement*, ed., David S. Dockery (Wheaton, Illinois: BridgePoint, 1995), 244-5.

Leighton G. Ford and Jim Denney, *The Power of Story:Rediscovering the Oldest, Most Natural Way to Reach People for Christ* (Colorado Springs: NavPress,1996).

creates a vision, which in turn creates character.[259] As Christians, we have been very demonstrative in proclaiming our morals to people who didn't share our story, and in many cases this has been counter-productive: not only has the world ignored us for the most part, we have also lost the hearing of many Gen X'ers who saw our preaching on morality as belligerence.[260] Many X'ers ask how we can we preach on morality, and condemn that which we see as immorality, when the people we are speaking against don't share our belief-system?

This question is inspired by the Postmodern understanding that right and wrong find their definition and origin in a worldview:

> Right and Wrong can thus only be discerned from *within* a particular tradition. Ethical action is dependent on indwelling a socially embodied narrative, on membership in a concrete community oriented to a distinctive perspective, heritage and vision of life. In MacIntyre's succinct formulation: "I can only answer the question "What am I to do?" if I can answer the prior question "Of what story or stories do I find myself part?"[261]

We can come to three conclusions here. The first is that it seems near futile to preach our morality to those who do not share our belief-system ("our story"). The fact of the matter is that in some very real ways Postmodern culture is trying to shed every remnant of Judeo-Christian culture, and in that context our sermonizing on morals is counter-

---

[259] Leighton G. Ford and Jim Denney, *The Power of Story - Rediscovering the Oldest, most Natural Way to Reach People for Christ* (Colorado Springs, CO: NavPress, 1994) 11.

[260] Long, 31.

[261] Richard J. Middleton and Brian J. Walsh, *Truth is Stranger Than It Used to Be* (Downers Grove, Illinois: Intervarsity Press, 1995), 216.

productive. If it is true that many people don't know the gospel anymore, then how can they ever understand the values of our morals?

Second, we must preach the morality that logically stems from our story to those who do accept it. The Postmodern people who will turn to Christ are likely to have no clue of the morals that are derived from the story. They will bring their own set of morals, which will be based on a culture that was trying to shed every element of the Judeo-Christian worldview. As we educate them into the Christian story, we educate them into a different worldview, with different morals.

Third, to those who do not accept our morality, we must start by sharing the story, rather than preaching the morals that derive from it. Especially when the context in which we live is increasingly losing all moral moorings, it is important that the church would clearly educate its people as to the morals that are implicit and explicit to our beliefs.

Purpose

The loss of a sense of purpose in life has been a direct result of the Modern worldview. Science that tries to contain the whole world of truth has produced great material progress. Yet it offers no idea whatsoever what it is for. Such science leaves people rich and powerful, but purposeless.[262] As Weber noted, rationalization can make the world orderly and reliable, but it cannot make the world meaningful.[263] There is then a loss of significance, or meaning, felt by people today. The gospel answers

---

[262] Tim Stafford, "God's Missionary to Us," *Christianity Today*, 40 (December 9, 1996), 26.

[263] James D. Hunter, "What is Modernity? Historical roots and contemporary features", *Faith and Modernity*, eds. Philip Sampson, Vinay Samual, Chris Sugden (Oxford, United Kingdom: Regnum. Books, 1994), 22.

existential questions and an apologetic that utilizes this insight would have to meet with a degree of interest.

The Sovereignty of God

With the demise of the belief in the Enlightenment project there also came an end to the trust in man's ability to solve every problem and nullify every threat. Instead, more than ever there is a sense of "it's a jungle out there" and in the future maybe not even the fittest will survive. Doomsday movies such as *Armageddon* and *Deep Impact* serve to heighten the awareness of the fragility of human life, or, for that matter, any life.

> Even for inattentive watchers, the unceasing [televised] display of misery and of experts endlessly disputing creates a sense of disarray. Feeling not "compassion fatigue" but inadequacy in the face of cognitive overload, they may realize (at some critical mass of incoherence) that things are beyond their control and the watchers feel abandoned by the civic world. But if they come to see that things are beyond anyone's control, then they are even more lost, and an even larger crisis of confidence can be anticipated.[264]

The message that God is very much in control, then, should very much be a good and comforting message to Postmodern ears. If in fact, we are not alone in the universe, and if everything, from the hairs on our head to the heavenly bodies in the sky, is in God's hands, then there is a reason to look at the future with expectation, hope, and even joy. To Postmodern ears the message that we live in a fallen world, but that Jesus will make all things new, should sound inspiring.

---

[264] Fitzgerald, Ibid.

Use of Technology

Having grown up in an age in which every area of life has been radically affected by technology, Postmodern people have a low tolerance for outdated and antiquated tools. The use of outdated technology by the church confirms to unchurched people that the church is hopelessly out of touch. Conversely, use of current technology raises the possibility that the church is not as outdated as originally expected, and may well deserve a second look.[265]

Embracing the Scriptures

Christians have always embraced the Bible as "their story." However, as the Bible came under investigation from skeptical Modernists Christians became defensive, and this has not escaped the world's attention. We have formulated various defenses to uphold the truthfulness and authority of the Bible. In the Postmodern era such defensiveness only leads to further suspicion of our claims. As Nash writes:

> But our very insistence upon the believability of the Bible is the first step toward rendering the Bible impotent. Among all the holy books of the world's religions, the Bible stands alone as the book that seems most threatened by serious scholarly challenge to its authenticity. My conversations with Muslims, Hindus, and Buddhists lead me to conclude that these persons do not feel similarly threatened by scholarly assessment of the Koran or Bhagavad Gita or the Dhammapada.

---

[265] Interesting in this respect is the multi-sensory perception church service, as advocated by Michael Slaughter. Michael Slaughter, *Out on the Edge: A Wake-Up Call for Church Leaders on the Edge of the Media Reformation* (Nashville, Tennessee: Abingdon Press, 1998).

Why not? Perhaps it is because faithful Muslims and Hindus and Buddhists consider such challenges to be insignificant. Their holy books serve as the sources for the stories that shape their lives. Scholars can dissect away; it really does not matter. The stories of these faiths still holds true for those who believe them. Questions about the scientific verifiability of these books can hardly cause a ripple among the faithful.[266]

In the Postmodern world stories provide meaning and significance while science is relegated to a less distinguished place than it had in the Modern world.[267] The Biblical story needs no defense as a metanarrative; it stands on its own. It also does not require a Modern defense, which is unfortunately, what some evangelicals have displayed, which has only raised eyebrows in the Postmodern world. The best defense of the Bible, in Postmodern eyes, is if we do what it preaches.[268]

This chapter has sought to delineate some of the values that will aid in making a ministry more conducive to reach successfully Postmoderns. This list is not complete in any way. Undoubtedly some will wish to add to, or take away from this list. We now turn our attention to necessary values and characteristics of churches in the Postmodern era.

---

[266] Nash, 68.

[267] See for instance Lee Campbell, "Postmodern Impact: Science" in Dennis McCallum, ed., *The Death of Truth* (Minneapolis, Minnesota: Bethany Publishers, 1996) 178-194.

[268] This is not to say that we should not stand for the historicity of the Bible. To Postmoderns historicity may initially not be "such a big deal" (perhaps they resemble liberal theology that way), but in time they will come to understand that historicity is important: it matters greatly that what we believe is indeed historically true.

Chapter 7 Churches that Reach Postmodern People

Rediscovering Biblical Christianity

Throughout the ages, the church has undergone profound changes. Every time the dominant worldview changed, war broke out or ended, new powers came to be, new styles became popular, and different theologies prevailed, the church changed. In every situation, Christians sought to be faithful to Scripture, while facing the challenges their world posed to them.

Now it is clear that the world in which we live has changed, and that the church if its message would remain relevant and intelligible, has to respond to these changes. Postmodernism poses two challenges that the church must face. First, the people the church is seeking to reach are changing. As demonstrated previously, ways of reaching people that were successful heretofore, are rapidly losing their effectiveness. Secondly, the emergence of the Postmodern worldview reveals the extent to which Modernism did influence the church. Obvious modernist influences on Christianity are an emphasis on the individual at the expense of the community, and an emphasis on the rational ability of human beings, at the expense of spiritual and emotional nature. Postmodernism helps the church to see its shortfalls in areas such as these. The church, if it is to be an effective witness to Christ in the Postmodern context, must recalibrate itself correspondingly. The point is not that the church must become Postmodern, but that Postmodernism helps the church to rediscover biblical Christianity. What must the church do to engage successfully Postmodern people? To what areas should church leadership pay special attention?

Community

Churches that desire to reach Postmodern people need to move beyond the individualism that characterized Modernism.[269] God's Kingdom is a communal Kingdom, and the church must be an expression of that in every way that it can. People need this community. They need a community that offers a grand reason for human existence ~ a community that will help them make sense of their experiences. [270] Postmodernists say that meaning can only be determined from within an "interpretive community." For Christians, the church is their interpretive community.[271]

The church must be a community that offers love, friendship, forgiveness, and cleansing. Such a community will take a central place in people's lives, "If people are embedded in such a community, then it can serve as the center from which they make sense of their lives. It should be more than just one of the many things they do. It should be the community out of which and for which they do everything."[272]

Mahedy and Bernardi also advocate that the church move beyond individualism to community. Their complaint is that Christianity has purposefully become a civil religion since Constantine, A.D. 312. Instead of being a community of believers, the Church (at large) has sought to be a

---

[269] Stanley J. Grenz, *Primer on Postmodernism* (Grand Rapids, Michigan: Eerchnans, 1996), 168.

[270] Robert N. Nash, Jr., An 8-Track Church in a CD World (Macon, Georgia: Smyth & Heiwys Publishing, 1997), 108.

[271] Michael Glodo, "The Bible in Stereo: New Opportunities for Biblical Interpretation in an A-Rational Age" in *The Challenge of Postmodernism - An Evangelical Engagement*, ed., David S. Dockery (Wheaton, Illinois: BridgePoint, 1995), 168. Not only is the church the interpretive community for Christians, but it seems logical that the church should endeavor to be the interpretive community for the world also. This is analogous to Paul's attempt to relate to the altar with the inscription "to the unknown God" (Acts 17).

[272] Nash, Ibid.

political player, a party of influence, and an authority in the world. Mahedy and Bernardi plead for the church to become "post-Constantinian". Constantinian Christianity brought war, crusades, persecutions and inquisitions, while the pre-Constantine church was well-known for its love for its members, care for the poor and radical witness to Christ. The Postmodern context demands that the church give up its pursuit of political power in whatever form, and instead pursue being a community of believers who love and care for each other, and for those in the world around them.[273]

In fact, many authors would agree, community is the best apologetic for the Postmodern age. "The greatest apologetic for the gospel" writes Brian McLaren, "is and always has been a community that actually lives by the gospel."[274]

When we discuss community, two issues often become the topic of conversation. They are unity and diversity, and the tension between them.

Unity

An important aspect of community is unity. Without unity there can be no community. Without unity, we have little to offer that the world does not already have.[275] The (essentially modernist) pursuit of truth is often perceived as being divisive. As we saw in chapter 2, one of the reasons people exchanged the Modern worldview for the Postmodern worldview, was the realization that there

---

[273] William Mahedy and Janet Bernardi, *A Generation Alone - X'ers Making a Place in the World* (Downer grove, Illinois, IVP Press, 1994), 48-51.

[274] Brian McLaren, *Reinventing your Church* (Grand Rapids, Michigan: Zondervan, 1998), 191. See also Lesslie Newbigin, *The Gospel in a Pluralist Society*, (Grand Rapids, Michigan: Eerdmans Publishing Company, 1989), 22.

[275] James Emery White, "Evangelism in a Postmodern World," in *The Challenge of Postmodernism - An Evangelical Engagement*, ed., David S. Dockery (Wheaton, Illinois: BridgePoint, 1995), 368-9.

would never be an agreement on truth, but that opinions about truth would continue to divide forever, sometimes with catastrophic results. Consequently, Postmodernists are quick to pick up on disagreements over correct dogma.

While truth is important, many Christians in the Postmodern era have a sense of regret at the many divisions in Christendom today, and their desire is to live differently. While the word "ecumenism" is not a popular one among all evangelicals, there is a search today for platforms for worship, prayer and evangelism together. Christians meet each other in inter-denominational organizations, conferences, television programs and magazines, and through interacting they are discovering each other as brothers and sisters. There are two growing sentiments today. One is "What binds us together, is greater than that which divides us." The other is that we have allowed doctrinal differences to divide us for too long, especially over issues that are now considered not quite important enough. Maybe it is the influence of Postmodernism in the church that we are now learning to appreciate diversity rather than seek total uniformity. In any case, these two sentiments are driving Christians and churches everywhere to pursue an ecumenicity of the heart.[276]

There is, of course, a valid concern over doctrine. Some issues must be worth separating over, or else our faith becomes utterly relative. There is a dividing line somewhere, but it would seem that Christians in the twenty-first century are putting it slightly to the left of where Christians in previous generations might have put it. Where the line belongs is a subject for discussion elsewhere, and one may be certain that there will be disagreement over it.

---

[276] See Dennis Miller, *Reinventing American Protestantism* (Berkeley, CA: University of California Press, 1997) 127-9.

Diversity

An equally important element of community, especially in the Postmodern era, is diversity. The Postmodern dream of creating a community or society in which people of many different walks-of-life, beliefs, and race can peacefully live together, bears a resemblance to what the church is supposed to be.[277] Sadly, under the influence of Modernism, the church displayed more homogeneity than diversity, creating stereotypes that, to the Postmodern world, are unattractive. Sunday morning is sadly the most racially segregated time of the week and intuitively Postmodern people sense this is in conflict with our message of reconciliation.[278]

In the Postmodern era, people expect that the church with its message of reconciliation and redemption will display colorfulness in every way. They expect the Church to reflect society, at least in terms of racial diversity. If the church becomes a place where people of diverse ethnicities are not welcome, the message is immediately discredited.

A similar issue plays in relationship to the way the Postmodern world perceives our stance towards the gay community. Could it be that we need to reassess to what extent our programs actually shun members of minority-groups? Some churches have started investigating ways to express Jesus' welcoming attitude without compromising his message.

This is not to say that the church should adopt theological pluriformity. But the church should be careful not to adopt a Pharisaic attitude, but rather the attitude of Jesus, who was accused of being a friend of tax-collectors and sinners. (Matt. 9:11-12) Perhaps it is not so much a

---

[277] See e.g. Eph. 2:14-18; Col. 3:11-14 and Rev. 7:9.

[278] George Barna, *The Second Coming of the Church* (Nashville, Tennessee: Word Publishing, 1998), 53.

matter of changing our doctrine regarding visitors and strangers, as it is a matter of putting what we actually believe into practice.

It is important that the church would make every effort to be such a community. Every single author on the topic of Postmodernism and the church emphasizes that postmodern people look for community, that they desperately need community. The church has a tremendous opportunity in the Postmodern context to extend the love of Christ by being the community he intended.[279]

Service According to Gifting and Calling

Whereas many churches have always understood the principle of the priesthood of all believers other churches, which perhaps emphasized a distinction between clergy and laity, are discovering (perhaps "rediscovering") this biblical truth.[280] Ministry, we are learning, is not the exclusive domain of trained experts; it is, in fact, the privilege of every Christian to serve Christ and his cause by discovering and utilizing his or her unique gifting. Following Ephesians 4:11-13 we now understand the role of those in full-time ministry to be to equip and prepare everyone in the church for "works of service."

It is important that we hold onto this understanding in the Postmodern era. Since Postmodernists exhibit a non-

---

[279] It is therefore very sobering to read that secular people seldom find community in the contemporary church. See e.g. James Emrry White, "Evangelism in a Postmodern World," in *The Challenge of Postmodernism - An Evangelical Engagement*, ed., David S. Dockery (Wheaton, Illinois: BridgePoint, 1995), 368-373.

[280] George G. Hunter III, *Church for the Unchurched* (Nashville, Tennessee: Abingdon Press, 1996) 32, 119-147.

ecclesial orientation, the role of the "laity" is critical in communicating the Christian message to them.[281]

We should begin to understand, not that the church has no clergy but rather that it has no laity! The similarities to the situation of the first century are striking in this sense. Postmodern pluralism strongly resembles the pluralism of Greek-Roman culture; Christianity was a small movement, a minority, a cult on the fringe of society; and, as James Hunter points out, early Christianity was *a lay movement*. No one was ordained in the sense of the word as we use it today.[282] It is therefore important that we constantly seek to empower and release the members of the church to minister.[283]

Team Ministry

In the light of the previous, it will come as no surprise that Team ministry is increasingly important. The awareness that "no man is an island", and no single individual has all that it takes, added to the fact that postmodern people find a large part of their own identity in the groups they are part of, makes team-ministry the *modus operandi*. The benefits of team ministry are many. Of great importance are:

- A spread of gifts and division of responsibilities.

- The ability to strengthen and encourage one another.

---

[281] Rick Gosnell, "Proclamation and the Postmodernist," in *The Challenge of Postmodernism -An Evangelical Engagement*, ed., David S. Dockery (Wheaton, Illinois: BridgePoint, 1995), 377.

[282] Hunter, 120.

[283] See David Hopkins, "Superman is dead: No more 'hero-for-hire' clergy", NEXT WAVE (April 1999) at http://www.next-wave.org/apr99/superman.htm.

- Interracial ministry. As cities across the world become increasingly ethnically diverse, and the Postmodern culture around us values integration and seeks to break down racial segregation, we must embrace each other across barriers of race, and work together. In this respect Postmodern culture is emphasizing what Christ showed us to do long ago, but we were slow to do. Evangelicalism in Europe and the U.S. / Canada today is predominantly a white Caucasian movement. In an era in which being white may be associated with being the oppressor or ruler, victimizing non-whites, evangelicalism is still monolithically white.[284]

Small Groups

There are two reasons small groups are important for the church in the Postmodern era. The first reason is that they are biblical. The early church met in homes everywhere. As James Hunter says, "The [Christian] movement not only seems to have planted small house churches wherever it spread, it also appears to have intentionally multiplied house churches in each city it reached. The small group was an essential structure for early Christianity."[285]

The second reason small groups are important is that they are instruments in fulfilling the need for community. They are an expression of the community we want to be. We grow together as we worship together, learn from each other, share each other's lives, build friendships, and minister to each other. Small groups are an effective environment for ongoing discipleship. "While the seeker

---

[284] Gene Edward Veith, Jr., *Postmodern Times - A Christian Guide to Contemporary Thought and Culture* (Wheaton, Illinois: Crossway Books, 1994), 162.

[285] Hunter, 82-3.

service may provide an initial introduction to the church or Christian fellowship, X'ers need to be invited into a more intimate community almost immediately."[286] They want to dialogue, while Boomers wanted to sit back and observe, carefully analyzing. Postmoderns realize that real knowledge only comes through participation. Small groups offer the ideal forum for that.

Preaching

As in any generation, preaching is a major function of the church. It is the proclamation of God's Word to God's people and the people of the world. Of course, this is no different in the Postmodern era. What is different, however, is that Postmodernism brings us additional understanding of the function of preaching in relation to the audience. We can see preaching in biblical terms of the proclamation of God's Word, much as Paul does (1 Corinthians 15:1-4). Concurrently, we can also look at preaching in sociological terms, in which the proclamation of the gospel becomes "the task of construing a reality, of telling people the way the world really is, of ordering people's perception around the throne of God."[287] Postmodernism helps us understand that preaching is more than proclamation; it is the construction of a reality in the mind's eye.

Preaching in the Postmodern era is different from preaching in the Modern era, because the audience is different. Changes have occurred in a number of ways. Postmodern people process information differently. They have a different worldview. They have a different view of religion, truth, themselves. The new context demands that we adapt, much as Paul did (1 Corinthians 9:22, 23) and as

---

[286] Jimmy Long, *Generating Hope - A Strategy for Reaching the Postmodern Generation* (Downer's Grove, Illinois: InterVarsity Press, 1997), 156.

[287] Glodo, 152.

he displayed at the Areopagus (Acts 17). The important question we need to ask ourselves is: How do you communicate God's Word effectively to people with a Postmodern mindset?[288]

Clear Biblical Peaching

There is a need for clear biblical teaching in the Postmodern age. The process of secularization has brought us to society in which there is very little left of the Judeo-Christian worldview. Western societies are increasingly moving from being Post-Christian to being Pre-Christian. In the Post-Christian society, there, at least, is a remnant of biblical understanding. Today, this is no longer the case: there is not even a memory of the hope-giving gospel.[289] Or, as Blaisdell puts it: "Scripture and tradition are penetrating conversation partners. However, for most postmoderns they are lost conversation partners. A huge part of the preacher's task in the postmodern world is to reintroduce them into the dialogue."[290] This means that there often is no God-concept to refer to. The contemporary preacher will need to do more groundwork. Much time will be spent establishing fundamentals. The biblical teaching will need to replace the secular worldview and understanding that people have. In those areas of life where the contemporary preacher fails to communicate

---

[288] An important question in this respect is the source of authority for preaching. In the Postmodern ethos there is no room for foundationalism, such as the belief that the Bible is the Word of God, and that it therefore is the foundation for preaching. This is a large discussion in itself, and it falls outside the scope of this work. See Alistair McGrath, *A Passion for Truth - The Intellectual Coherence of Evangelicalism* (Downers Grove, Illinois: Intervarsity Press, 1996) for more on this subject.

[289] Andres Tapia, "Generation X", *Christianity Today* (September 12, 1994), 18.

[290] Barbara Blaisdell in Ronald J. Allen, Barbara Shires Blaisdell and. Scott Black Johnston, *Theology for Preaching - Authority, Truth and Knowledge of God in a Postmodern Ethos* (Nashville, Tennessee: Abingdon Press, 1997), 47-8.

biblical truth, the original secular worldview is likely to remain intact. To the extent that biblical teaching is not given, the thought-structures of Postmodern culture will remain present. This means that if a preacher does not explain the implications of the Christian worldview on sexuality, worldly ideas about sexuality will remain in place, together with corresponding practice. Likewise, to the extent that churches fail to speak on the implications of the Christian worldview for marriage, people will fail to build marriages that are biblical and healthy.

One of the challenges that the Postmodernism worldview poses is that its doctrine is discovered by experience. "If it feels good, do it," becomes the philosophy of life: "If it feels good, it must be all right", or "it must be true." Such a method of discovering truth is of course fundamentally a non-biblical epistemology. The Postmodern context puts the demand on preaching that we establish God's truth as revealed in His Word, constantly seeking to renew the mind of our audience, by substituting the truth of this world with the truth from God's Word.

Narrative

In the Modern era, there was a delight in distilling truth into principles and propositions. Truth and values were best conveyed in short sentences that were open to empirical investigation, and could be proved to be either true or false. Preaching became theological discussion. Postmodernists critique this Modern approach for being reductionist. Observing how cultures the world over use stories to convey meaning, values, morals, principles and truths, Postmodernist believe that, while the Modern approach engaged only the mind, stories, in fact, engage both the mind and the heart. In the Postmodern perspective, it not only matters what truth you tell, but also how you say it ~ making details of context and infrastructure suddenly relevant. The story contains the theology, the values and the explanation of reality. But instead of merely engaging the mind, it also engages the heart and the spirit, creating a compelling appeal to its audience.

Philip Yancey, in his best-selling book *What's so Amazing About Grace*, gives a great example of how mere facts and propositions can present the subject without any incentive to change whereas stories create that incentive.

> Grace does not offer an easy subject for a writer. To borrow E. B. White's comment about humor, "[Grace] can be dissected, as a frog, but the thing dies in the process, and the innards are discouraging to any but the pure scientific mind." I have just read a thirteen-page treatise on grace...which has cured me of any desire to dissect grace and display its innards. I do not want the thing to die. For this reason, I will rely more on stories than on syllogisms.
>
> In sum, I would far rather convey grace than explain it.[291]

In the Postmodern world there is an emphasis on Narrative. Everyone has a story, and that story conveys beliefs, values, and passions. Truth is conveyed not in a propositional manner, but through narrative. Because of this mindset, there is a great openness to stories. This generation will not listen to dogmatic discourse, but they will listen to any good story.[292]

---

[291] Philip Yancey, *What's so Amazing About Grace?* (Grand Rapids, Michigan: Zondervan Publishing House, 1997), 16.

[292] For the sake of the argument I make a distinction between narrative preaching and propositional preaching stronger than it really exists. While the basic distinction is valid, there are of course many shades of grey between black and white, to use an analogy. Furthermore, it can also be said that stories can, and often do, contain an amount of propositional teaching. Jesus' parables are a case in point; they were not meant merely to entertain, but to teach and give insight.

This is an interesting characteristic of Postmodernism. There are those who wonder if evangelicals have not violated the nature of God's Word in attempting to distil truth into systems of doctrine and theology.[293] While it cannot be denied that such an approach has been fruitful in helping our understanding of what the Bible says, it must be asked if such an approach was reductionist. "God has entrusted us, His Church, with the best story in the world", writes Stanley Hauerwas. "With great ingenuity we have managed, with the aid of much theory, to make that story boring as hell."[294]

Postmodern Christians are quick to point out that much of the Bible is narrative, and that even Romans, held by many to be the purest theology the Bible has, is situational in nature, and refers over and over to narrative.[295] As Christians, we have the greatest story ever told. The story of God's love, search for, and the pursuit of mankind is more powerful than any other. That story conveys our beliefs, our values, and our passions.

The Gospel has an irreducibly narrative structure. It is a story not a set of disembodied truths or theological propositions. The meaning of a story is always greater than can be captured by

---

For more on this see Henry H. Knight, *A Future for Truth - Evangelical Theology in a Postmodern World* (Nashville, Tennessee: Abingdon Press, 1997).

[293] See e.g. Nash, Long, Richard J. Middleton and Brian J. Walsh, *Truth is Stranger Than It Used to Be* (Downers Grove, Illinois: Intervarsity Press, 1995), and D.A Carson, *The Gagging of God* (Grand Rapids, Michigan: Zondervan, 1996).

[294] Stanley Hauerwas, "Preaching as Though We Had Enemies," *First Things* 53, (May 1995).

[295] See Rom 1:18-32, 4:1-25, 5:12-15, 8:18-26, 9:1-33, 11:1-10, 11:25-32, 15:23-29. Besides quoting from the Old Testament numerous times, and using examples such as marriage to get his point across, Romans provides much of the narrative of the Christian story, all the way from the Creation and Fall (chapter 1) to the return of Christ and the Redemption of Israel. To view Romans as pure systematic theology seems inaccurate.

any attempt to reduce it to propositional form. Thus, the gospel cannot be articulated exhaustively as a system of doctrine. Similarly, it cannot be programmatic.[296]

A bold proclamation of the Bible story, especially of the historical life, death, and resurrection of Jesus, is the central authority for Christian preaching. Regardless of place or time, the story of the gospel is the core of the Christian message and the reason for our preaching.

> Our theology is ultimately a story. It is a story of hope in the midst of brokenness. We live out our story in a world that is broken, in broken relationships, with broken promises. We tell a story where the Creator has become the Repairman. He is sewing together the world that has ripped apart. He is piecing together relationships. He is making promises that, despite the bleak outlook, he makes good by the end of the story. He comes through! Like any good story, we don't see how we will make it, but we hope against hope. As we shall see, we have hope that does not disappoint us.[297]

To reach people in the Postmodern world it must be clear that a principle-based apologetic will tend not to be effective, and that there is a need for a story-driven apologetic. Kevin Ford advocates such a story-driven approach. He writes:

...the Christian story unlocks a number of gateways to the soul of Generation X. Some examples:

---

[296] Lawrence Osborn, "Collision Crossroads: The Intersection of Modern Western Culture with the Christian Gospel," *The Gospel and Culture*, ed. J. Flat (Auckland: The DeepSight Trust, 1998), 34-39.

[297] Todd Hahn and David Verhaagen, *Reckless Hope - Understanding and Reaching Baby-Busters* (Grand Rapids, Michigan: Baker Book House, 1996), 60.

- X'ers are alienated. The Christian story brings reconciliation.

- X'ers feel betrayed. The Christian story brings promise and restores broken trust.

- X'ers feel vulnerable and insecure. The Christian story brings a sense of safety within a protective healing, community.

- X'ers lack defined identity. The Christian story gives them a new identity in Christ.

- X'ers have been burned by pathological models of authority. The Christian story reveals an authority that is positive, not pathological.

X'ers feel unwanted and unneeded. The Christian story offers them a place of belonging, a place for involvement, a place where their lives can be used in service of a purpose that is larger than themselves.[298]

"Don't destroy a good narrative by breaking it up with points," says Kevin Ford. "That's condescending. Just tell a story. And don't explain it."[299]

Don't explain it? That may seem rather dangerous to many evangelicals. Isn't that what preachers do? Isn't that what the study of hermeneutics is all about? Perhaps it is but balance is restored by sometimes erring too far in the opposite direction, and it is time we allowed the story to stand on its own. It does not need our explanation. Ford demonstrates the need for further growth and exploration of narrative preaching.[300]

---

[298] Kevin Ford, *Jesus for a New Generation* (Downer's Grove, Illinois: InterVarsity Press, 1995), 173.

[299] Kevin Ford, *LEADERSHIP*, journal. Fall 1996, Vol. XVII, No. 4, Page 17.

[300] There is a distinction between narrative preaching and narrative theology. While the first can be defined as preaching the story for its full impact,

145

Ambiguity

While there is a need for clear biblical teaching, Postmodern people also desire that a preacher be open and honest about those issues which he doesn't understand. "The preacher cannot always step into the pulpit with a sermon bearing the unqualified imprint, 'thus saith the Lord,'" says Ron Allen. "Life and Christian perception do not always fall into clearly defined categories."[301] This awareness causes Postmodern people to resist any cut-and-dried approach to reality and life. They understand that no one person can understand everything and have an answer for every question, and to suggest that one does, is simply to display a lack of honesty and authenticity. To the Postmodern mind, an honest statement of ambiguity actually contributes to the preacher's credibility.[302]

Moreover, such an attitude reflects the honesty that is so important. Under the influence of Modernism the preacher often adopted the role of the one with all the answers. But Postmodern people realize that no one person has a hold on the truth: "we never have a complete, sure,

---

the second is a school of theology with which evangelicals feel a certain amount of tension. In recommending narrative preaching I am not advocating narrative theology. Narrative theology, of which George Lindbeck is one of the chief proponents, studies the narrative nature of the story, and its impact today, without addressing the question of historicity. While we can benefit from insights in narrative theology, such as the study of literary forms, the issue of historicity clearly is important to how we understand the text.

[301] Ronald J. Allen, Barbara Shires Blaisdell and Scott Black Johnston, *Theology for Preaching - Authority, Truth and Knowledge of God in a Postmodern Ethos* (Nashville, Tennessee: Abingdon Press, 1997), 42-43.

[302] Ibid.

or untainted knowledge of any concept or person, nor do we have such knowledge of God."[303]

To evangelicals this may seem like a troubling notion. If we can never know anything absolutely, how can we know God at all? Johnston says:

> We must remember that Moses, with his face pressed firmly into a mountain crevice by the hand of the Almighty, was able to only catch a reflected glint of God's passing glory. Indeed, Moses is protected from having a more direct encounter with his Creator, for as God informs him, full access to the face of the divine would surely prove fatal. Preachers should detect a note of caution in this ancient theophany. Attempts to convey the fullness of God in our sermons are ultimately futile and actually undesirable; for full knowledge of the divine is something that finite beings are neither able to convey nor equipped to handle.[304]

Conversation and Dialogue

There are three reasons why discussion, conversation and dialogue are important ministry tools in the Postmodern age. The Postmodern ethos questions the infallibility of the teacher. They want to explore together rather than have things explained to them by experts. Expert facilitation in a group dynamics context is acceptable but there is a dislike for the didactic, "I'm the oracle of wisdom and you are the empty vessels" attitude. While Postmoderns are willing to consider everything and anything, they want to be able to ask questions and have discussion. This is because learning in the Postmodern age is

---

[303] Ronald J. Allen, Barbara Shires Blaisdell and Scott Black Johnston, *Theology for Preaching - Authority, Truth and Knowledge of God in a Postmodern Ethos* (Nashville, Tennessee: Abingdon Press, 1997), 102.

[304] Ibid.

experienced in an egalitarian manner where issues are explored rather than explained. Certainly, the pastor is likely to be regarded as a man with wisdom that can be of benefit but he will be expected to elicit rather than instill truth. Therefore, it is really a matter of how he facilitates the learning process.

Another reason that discussion and dialogue are important in the postmodern age is that Postmodern people receive so much information that they sometimes have trouble making sense of all the data. Conversation and dialogue are important because it helps people process the information. Discussion and dialogue creates the occasion for critical reflection that helps them discern alternative interpretations of the data and the positive and negative qualities of each.[305]

The last reason discussion and dialogue are important is that Postmodern people crave respect. The Postmodern worldview holds that worldviews are intolerant of each other by definition, and this intolerance is unpardonable in postmodern thinking. It is for this reason that mere proclamation of truth will not yield the same result is has for decades. Postmodern people simply will not give us a hearing when we cannot convey basic respect for those of other convictions. This is why dialogue is such an important ministry tool. It gives us the opportunity to understand the other person. That search for understanding of the other person conveys to Postmodern people the respect they desire.

Practical

Many people have left the church because what they were taught was irrelevant to their lives. Treatises on the correct form of baptism or the right eschatology simply did

---

[305] Op. Cit. 41.

not provide people with the spiritual guidance for everyday life they so desperately needed. Postmodern people are drawn to churches "in which worship is caring and relational and in which the truth of the Bible rests not in propositional assertions about God but rather in applications to the daily struggles of life."[306]

There is a need for churches to reassess their values, their style, and their programs. This chapter has sought to comment on some of the most important issues that churches with a desire to reach postmodern people will need to deal with. The next chapter turns to that essential part of church life we call "worship."

---

[306] Nash, 63.

CHAPTER 8 Worship In a Postmodern World

The very purpose for which we, and, by logical extension the church, were created, was to worship God. Worship is at the heart of our relationship to Christ. It is there that we encounter Him most intimately. It is there that we meet Him with our whole being. Worship, at least in a Biblical sense, is something we do with everything we have and are: spiritually, physically, musically, vocally, artistically, mentally and emotionally.

To the modern mind, the concept of worship of an invisible God was incomprehensible. To the Modern mindset, it was an awkward experience for non-Christians to encounter a Christian worship service, particularly if it was more expressive or spontaneous. The Postmodern mind regards our worship differently. Viewing Christians as a tribe, with its own culture, metanarrative, and language, Postmoderns are likely to experience less awkwardness and more curiosity.[307] In their eyes, the way we worship is an extension of our worldview, and "who are they to pass a verdict on it"?

If there is one area where we can demonstrate our desire to make the church a place where Postmodern seekers can feel welcome, it is in our worship.[308] It is here that we must do everything possible to assess the way we do things and the extent to which those ways still makes sense in the Postmodern context. Nash says:

---

[307] The subject of Tribalism was introduced in chapter 5 under the heading "craving community". It refers to the idea that people, who are bound together by one single meta-narrative, function as a tribe. This phenomenon is called "The New Tribalism" and it allows sociologists and anthropologists a certain amount of categorization of people. See Gene Edward Veith, Jr., *Postmodern Times - A Christian Guide to Contemporary Thought and Culture* (Wheaton, Illinois: Crossway Books, 1994), chapter 8.

[308] This might raise questions I am not addressing her about whether or not the purpose of worship can include an evangelistic dimension.

We live in an age of easy belief. Churches are surrounded by a culture that is radically pluralistic, highly spiritual, antidogmatic, and nonrational. In such a climate, there must be a rebirth of Christian spirituality. A new kind of Christianity must emerge that is exciting, unapologetic, confident, resourceful and courageous. It must be a Christianity that is freed from the modern approach to the faith that has dominated in the...church.[309]

At the same time, no area of church life has seen as much change and debate as the area of worship. Much of the conflict over worship has been over instruments (organ or guitar), choice of music (traditional, (contemporary, blended), and style (spontaneous or liturgical). Now the Postmodern context brings new challenges to our concept of worship.

The modern context has influenced our concept of worship, and the emergence of the Postmodern era reveals that influence. Worship, argues Gary Burge, has become too horizontal, too worldly.[310]

So what is worship? Worship, I believe, is a divine encounter that touches many dimensions of my personhood. It is an encounter, in which, God's glory, Word, and grace are unveiled, and we respond, in songs of prayer and celebration. Worshipers seek an encounter with the glory of God, the transcendent power and numinous mystery of the divine - and in so doing, they recognize a Lord whose majesty evokes praise, petition, and transformation.[311]

---

[309] Robert N. Nash, Jr., *An 8-Track Church in a CD World* (Macon, Georgia: Smyth & Helwys Publishing, 1997), 67.

[310] Gary M. Burge, "Are Evangelicals Missing God at Church?" *Christianity Today*, 6 October, 1997, 23.

[311] Op. Cit., 22.

It will take evangelicals some effort to design worship services that truly offer such an encounter with God. And yet, argues Burge, we must become the architects, because "it is through our craft [as pastors and worship leaders] that we will be able to enrich and build the spiritual lives of our people."[312] What will draw people to Christ is the beauty of God, as evidenced and exalted through creative worship, rather than an elaboration on the proofs of God's existence.[313]

The seeker-movement has focused long and hard on ways to make church accessible to seekers. A basic premise of the seeker movement is that seekers can experience something of God when churches make their worship understandable and intelligible and their worship style attractive. Today the seeker-movement is far from dead. While some authors have classified seeker-sensitive churches such as Willow Creek as typically Modern, in that they seem to be very mechanical, technocratic and principle-driven, more authors have said that seeker-churches will be the churches that are effective in bringing in the Postmodern harvest.[314] This stands to reason, as the basic premise of the seeker-movement is that you seek to understand your audience as best you can, and then develop a strategy that will be effective in affecting and winning that audience. Seeker-sensitive strategies are therefore different from one setting to the next, and such differences may be quite obvious, in worship style, in sermon themes, in organizational structure and in evangelistic strategy. However, the basic philosophy behind all is the same ~ God is a missionary God,

---

[312] Ibid.

[313] Michael J. Glodo, "The Bible in Stereo: New Opportunities for Biblical Interpretation in a A-Rational Age" in *The Challenge of Postmodernism - An Evangelical Engagement*, ed., David S. Dockery (Wheaton, Illinois: BridgePoint, 1995), 155. See also Pierre Babin with Mercedes Iannone, *The New Era   In Religious Communication* (Philadelphia: Fortress Press, 1991), 14.

[314] See James Emery White, "Evangelism in a Postmodern World," in *The Challenge of Postmodernism - An Evangelical Engagement*, ed., David S. Dockery (Wheaton, Illinois: BridgePoint, 1995), 368-9.

and, therefore, his people are a missionary people.[315] In addition, the first task of the missionary is contextualization of the message to the new context.[316]

A Focus on the Arts

No generation has been conditioned by image and sound as much as this one has. To the Postmodern mind, everything is image, and the image is everything. More powerful than words, communication in this generation happens through images. Because of this, many Christians are exploring ways to use film, photo/video, multi-media, painting/drawing/sketches, music, dance, drama, sculpting and other graphic forms of art to communicate the message. McLaren says, "We must rely more than ever on art, music, literature and drama to communicate our message."[317]

Creativity

Creativity is going to be key in reaching Postmodern people. As a result of the holistic view of the human being, the Modern emphasis solely on man's rational ability has been replaced by the desire to seek to unlock all of man's abilities, including the creative "right brain" functions. Creativity is furthermore important because so many of the ways we "do church" were designed long ago, and all too often form and content are being confused. To reach people in the Postmodern era we need to realize that while the content of the message never changes, every age needs the message

---

[315] David J. Bosch, *Believing in the Future - Toward a Missiology of Western Culture* (Valley Forge, Pennsylvania: Trinity Press International, 1995), 32.

[316] The publisher, Christian Publishing House, would recommend that the reader consider the following article,

Contextualization, Seeker-Movement, or Seeker Sensitive Methods of Evangelism =Nine Parts World to One Part Christian

http://www.christianpublishers.org/you-are-no-part-of-the-world

[317] Brian McLaren, *Reinventing Your Church* (Grand Rapids, Michigan: Zondervan, 1998), 33.

to be put in a new, relevant and understandable form. Creativity is thus a necessary element of contextualization.

The ever-present tension in contextualization is the danger that the form will somehow change the message. Wherever people have sought to introduce creative new ways of communicating the message, there are always those who feel the message is being compromised.

There have been many creative ways in which some churches have sought to reach out to people (especially young people) through the use of dance and technology. Christian Rock bands have emerged and Christians have used these as a way of engaging youth. There have been outdoor parties hosted by churches where firework displays have been used. Some churches have used wind machines and dry ice to produce an ambient experience during worship. Some churches have hosted art exhibitions of the works of its members and invited other artists to either participate in or witness the display. Some churches have engaged in meditation sessions, and others have read poetry. The list is endless, but these are a few innovative approaches.

I have preached in a church in Amsterdam called "Amsterdam 50". The service is held on Sunday afternoons at 4 pm in a bar that serves barista coffees ~ cappuccino, latte, Americano, herbal teas, fruit drinks, pastries, etc.). The furniture was arranged in cabaret style, with tables and chairs where people sat in small groups. There was a time of reverential worship and the people who were present (about 80, mostly in their 20s and 30s) listened attentively to the preaching. Do these new ways violate the message? No doubt some will say that they do, but I think not.

Experiencing God

Postmodern people desire to experience God. They have a hard time believing in something that they cannot experience. They have a desire to experience the transcendent. The Enlightenment, with its emphasis on reason and objective ways of explaining everything, perceived religion as superstition, a thing of the past.

154

The Enlightenment consistently ignored the supernatural realm. It is as if the Enlightenment created a vacuum that Postmodern people are now trying to fill.

Evangelicalism, influenced as it was by the Enlightenment, fell prey to the same trap. Though evangelicals professed a faith in the supernatural, their actual experience of it was minimized to professions of faith and the practice of some spiritual disciplines.[318] Elaborate theological frameworks were established to explain the absence of any experience of the supernatural in the present age.

The emergence of the Pentecostal and charismatic movements, followed by the Third Wave-movement, changed all that. Many view the emergence of these movements as the work of God, restoring to the church a vitality that had been lost. Others view them with disdain.[319] While the Pentecostal and charismatic movement were somewhat removed from the evangelical churches because of different beliefs concerning the baptism of the Holy Spirit, the Third Wave movement introduced the work of the Holy Spirit into many mainline evangelical churches. Though still regarded suspiciously by some, these movements can largely be held responsible for the reintroduction of the experience of the supernatural in normal life. "Many evangelicals," says Greig and Springer, "have begun to realize that biblical Christianity is much more than they had previously known."[320]

With that awareness the expectation that God in fact can and does move in mysterious ways is becoming more and more prevalent today. That is good, because a Christianity that can provide no experience of what it believes, will have a hard time being relevant in any way to Postmodern people.

---

[318] Kirk Bottomly, "Coming out of the Hangar - Confessions of a Christian Deist," *The Kingdom and the Power*, Gary S. Greig and Kevin N. Springer, eds. (Ventura, California: Regal Books, 1993), 279.

[319] See, for example, John MacArthur, *Strange Fire: The Danger of Offending the Holy Spirit with Counterfeit Worship*, Thomas Nelson, 2013. This is similar to his earlier work, *Charismatic Chaos*, Zondervan, 1993.

[320] Gary S. Greig and Kevin N. Springer, *The Kingdom and the Power* (Ventura, California: Regal Books, 1993), 21.

In this respect, it may be recognized that Postmodernism, with its desire for experience of the supernatural, is in fact helping restore an understanding of biblical Christianity to the church. Under the influence of the Enlightenment our understanding of the human being, if not in theory, then at least in practice, reflected that we perceived man to consist of body and mind. Stanley Grenz calls this dualistic and states his hope that the church will move beyond this dualism, "If we would minister in the Postmodern context, however, we must realize that the next generation is increasingly interested in the human person as a unified whole. The gospel we proclaim must speak to human beings in their entirety."[321] Christian worship is one of the primary places where Postmodern people can experience something of God.

Study Other Christian Traditions

In order to spark the quality of spirituality we need as church in the Postmodern era, Nash says we must draw from other Christian traditions and the full resources of Christian history.[322] This fits the Postmodern context, which is very interested in exploring ancient types of spirituality. This trait of Postmodern spirituality, some have observed, can easily become a mix-and-match of different kinds of spirituality from different eras. Be that as it may, Postmodern people believe they can benefit from exploring historical spiritual paths. While the desire to mix-and-match (to search in Christian history for usable elements) may be considered by some to be a questionable motive, the truth is we can benefit from this attitude in a couple of ways.

We share in the blessing of historical Christianity. By incorporating prayers, songs, themes and images from church history, we access some of the wonderful things the church has

---

[321] Stanley J. Grenz, *Primer on Postmodernism* (Grand Rapids, Michigan: Eerdmans, 1996), 63; D. A Carson, *The Gagging of God* (Grand Rapids, Michigan: Zondervan, 1996), 171.

[322] Robert N. Nash, Jr., *An 8-Track Church in a CD World* (Macon, Georgia: Smyth & Helwys Publishing, 1997), 74.

enjoyed over the centuries. We place ourselves in the Christian tradition, showing ourselves to be a historical faith. Our identification with historical Christianity places us solidly within the Christian tradition, which keeps us from being identified as a new cult or religious sect. We can cross denominational borders, and by doing so demonstrate our desire for unity and our recognition of the validity of the faith of those in other Christian traditions.

Meditation

An element of worship that seems to be particularly meaningful to contemporary people is meditation. This causes many evangelicals some discomfort, as the practice of meditation has been largely lost by evangelicals. Possibly it was the influence of rationalism that there was not much place in our churches for meditation.

In fact, many Christians today do not regard meditation as a Christian practice. They are ignorant of the fact that it was practiced throughout Christian history and many people today find meditation very meaningful. [323] It seems that somehow people have a sense of rediscovering their spiritual needs as they take time for quiet contemplation, silence, and withdrawal from the world.

It is reasonable to expect that the whole area of worship will undergo major changes in the coming years. Indeed, this process is already underway in many places. If a generation ago one selected a church on the basis of its theology and teaching, more and more people now select churches on the basis of its style. An ever growing variety of styles is available to them: different cultural flavors, varying styles of music, the use of multimedia, arts, dance, expressiveness ~ the church has already entered the Postmodern era. The next chapter will discuss how evangelism takes place in the Postmodern world.

---

[323] Nash, 75.

CHAPTER 9 Evangelism

While the church has found itself pursuing different objectives at different times, the ultimate mission of the church is found in Jesus' words: "Go therefore and make disciples of all the nations." (Matt. 28: 18-20) The mission of the church is to produce more and better disciples. The Postmodern context demands that we reconsider what evangelism is and how we do it. This chapter seeks to describe some of the changes that are necessary in our thinking.

A Biblical model of Conversion

We need a biblical model of conversion. Under the influence of Modernism the church had constructed a very narrow and precise definition of conversion. That concept, most evangelicals would contend, was based on Scripture. The Four Spiritual Laws approach, as made popular by Bill Bright and Campus Crusade for Christ, sought to "distil" the entire scriptural understanding of conversion into four easy, quickly understandable statements. As Christians wrestle with the Postmodern worldview, some are coming to the conclusion that such an approach had strongly modern features. As admirable as it may have been, the new Postmodern context challenges our concept of conversion and perhaps it is time we reconsidered what conversion really is. Kallenberg says incoherencies jeopardize the practice of evangelism in the conservative [evangelical] formulations of the doctrine of conversion.[324] The objective is not to come to a Postmodern understanding of conversion but rather to come to a biblical understanding of conversion that will incorporate insight from Postmodernism and that will effectively relate to the Postmodern context.

---

[324] Brad J. Kallenberg, "Conversion Converted: A Postmodern Formulation of the Doctrine of Conversion." *Evangelical Quarterly* 67:4 (1995): 335-364. Kallenberg examines the doctrine of conversion as formulated by Louis Berkhof, and writes: "I shall argue that his formulation of the doctrine is deficient in precisely the three ways he has presupposed modem philosophy." (p. 337).

So what was wrong with the Modern concept of conversion? Robert Nash writes:

> The very phrase "plan of salvation" smacks of a modern approach to sharing the Christian faith. It is neat, it is systematic, well-ordered, and efficient. It is designed to spread the gospel to the greatest amount of people in the shortest amount of time, which is certainly a modern goal if there ever was one! Plans of salvation such as the "Roman Road," the "Four Spiritual Laws," and other tract-like approaches to faith certainly served their purpose in modernity. Millions of people entered the Christian faith through just such a methodology...In the modern world, people accepted the notion that, to be a Christian, all one had to do was to "pray the sinner's prayer."[325]

In their attempt to interact with the Postmodern context a number of authors react to this concept of conversion rather negatively. It is the result of the Enlightenment that the word *belief* lost its original meaning, and came to refer merely to intellectual assent, writes Long.[326]

Intellectual assent to the basic tenets of faith is only one part of the journey toward God, says Nash.[327] True discipleship begins with the process of conversion and then moves beyond that into an intimate relationship with our Father in heaven, and integration into the community of the saints, both of which will ultimately culminate in heaven. To view conversion as a safeguard against a one-way trip to hell falls short of what the Christian life is all about.

The Modern approach to conversion was further evidenced in the factory-like method of disciple-making. It pumped Christians

---

[325] Robert N. Nash, Jr., *An 8-Track Church in a CD World* (Macon, Georgia: Smyth & Heiwys Publishing, 1997), 58-59.

[326] Jimmy Long, *Generating Hope - A Strategy for Reaching the Postmodern Generation* (Downer's Grove, Illinois: InterVarsity Press, 1997), 161.

[327] Nash, 63.

out in a kind of assembly line, writes Nash. Once you had been stamped with a date, you were sent out into the world to start new factories and produce more Christians. The goal was for people to avoid eternal punishment.[328] While Nash recognizes the validity of that attempt, he wonders if that is all there is to making disciples. Doesn't such a view of disciple-making fall short of the biblical concept? The pragmatic event of salvation allowed the new Christian to avoid something (namely, the fires of hell), rather than experience something (namely, a relationship with God).[329]

And the church encouraged this fear. It was, after all, the quickest and easiest way to bring people into the Kingdom of God. It worked quite well in a modern world in which people subscribed to a single Christian reality. Everyone believed in heaven, and everyone believed in hell. Being a pragmatic; modern institution, the church focused its time and energy on the strategy that worked. But, by focusing most of its attention on the eternal destination of its constituents, the church failed to give sufficient attention to enhancing the spiritual lives of its people.[330]

What then is a good approach to conversion? Kallenberg suggests that conversion is more than intellectual assent to certain propositions. He rephrases the doctrine so that conversion comes to mean the "emergence of a new mode of life occasioned by the self-involving participation in the shared life, language, and paradigm of the believing community."[331]

---

[328] Op. Cit. 59.

[329] This approach to conversion has come to be called the fire-insurance approach. The idea is the following. One never knows if one will have to endure a fire. One of course hopes not. But should there ever be a fire, then it is a good idea to have insurance just in case. Nash's view of organizations like Campus Crusade for Christ and Navigators is rather negative but Nash does not mention the many ways in which these organizations have brought a tremendous blessing.

[330] Op. Cit., 60.

[331] Kallenberg, 363.

A number of things stand out in this definition. First, conversion happens as one becomes involved with the community of believers. True conversion cannot really happen without the community of believers involved in some way.[332] Coming to Christ means one becomes part of the community of the saints. That community has a shared life and the individual person who converts to Christ, participates in that life.

This emphasis on community is a change from the modernist individualistic approach to conversion. That approach consistently put the individual outside of the community, making conversion a private matter between God and the individual. The result of that approach is that more people profess to believe in God than the number of people who attend church regularly. A common sentiment is that one doesn't need to be told what to believe by a pastor.

Second, this definition takes into account that the community has a language that is particular to that community. Language has reality-shaping power, Postmodernists hold.[333] Lindbeck says, "Stated more technically, a religion can be viewed as a kind of cultural and/or linguistic framework or medium that shapes the entirety of life and thought."[334] This moves Lindbeck to state:

> The Christian theological application of this view is that just as an individual becomes human by learning a language, so he or she becomes a Christian through hearing and interiorizing the language that speaks of Christ.[335]

---

[332] If nothing else, conversion places one in the body of Christ, which is a community.

[333] A concept that, says Kallenberg, has strong theological precedent. The priority of the Word in Scripture is evidenced in creation, Jesus' healings, and in John's gospel where Jesus is spoken of as the Word of God. Kallenberg, 350.

[334] George A. Lindbeck, *The Nature of Doctrine* (Philadelphia, PA: Westminster Press, 1984), 33. Quoted by Kallenberg, 335-364.

[335] Op. Cit., 62. Lindbeck's statement, admittedly, is more Darwinian than Scriptural. Yet it explains one of the dynamics in conversion quite helpfully.

Kallenberg adds, "part and parcel of becoming an insider is learning to speak the language so that Jesus' teaching can be heard and understood on its own terms...Language instruction, therefore, is a central part of evangelism." This conclusion causes Kallenberg to call for evangelism that is pedagogical in nature. Evangelism is teaching others about Christ, using the language of faith to instruct others in the faith.[336]

Third, the individual undergoes a paradigm shift as he enters the community. The process of conversion is the process in which the secular worldview is replaced by the Christian worldview. Whether this process happens fast or slow, this paradigm shift is an essential part of the conversion process.

As we have seen, Postmodernists ultimately regard a worldview as a story. Kallenberg, pointing at the narrative nature of much of Scripture, does not consider that inappropriate. He encourages us to tell the stories of the gospel often and well. Because, says Kallenberg, faith comes by hearing, and hearing by the Word of God (Romans 10:17). In the end, it is the story that people have to believe. They have to "buy in." They must buy into the story, into the community, and into the language.

Like Kallenberg, Jimmy Long attempts to uncover a biblical approach to conversion. "For the sake of our witness and for the sake of Christian formation, we need to recover the original meaning of the word *believe*, that is, to trust, rely and obey."[337]

Conversion is the process of putting trust in Christ. But now Postmodernism has opened our eyes to the fact that any worldview requires faith, even a purely technical/Modernist one. Even science, properly understood, is based on faith commitments and the scientific community is fiduciary in this sense, as has been demonstrated by Michael Polanyi in, for example, *Personal Knowledge*. Taking his cue from Polanyi, Newbigin writes that

---

[336] Kallenberg, 360.

[337] Long, 161, cf Rudolf Bultmann, "Pistueo," in *Theological Dictionary of the New Testament*, abridged ed., (Grand Rapids, Michigan: Eerdmans, 1985), 853. We will return to Jimmy Long's concept of conversion in the next section.

there is "no knowing without believing". Newbigin maintains that all truth, scientific or religious, fact or value, is arrived at by a common route. This begins with a "fiduciary act" and leads, through commitment and even passion for discovery, to "personal knowledge", which is the title of Polanyi's work to which Newbigin pays tribute.[338]

Writing on the church in the Postmodern era Grenz states that the church needs to become "post-dualistic." The dualism he refers to was an element of Modernism that crept into the church. It made a distinction between "mind" and "matter". This fundamental dualism, he writes, affected the Enlightenment view of the human person as "soul" (thinking substance) and "body" (physical substance). This distinction entered the church and impacted the gospel it preached. Rather than emphasizing how the gospel is good for the whole person, the emphasis was on "saving souls."

If we would minister in the Postmodern context, however, we must realize that the next generation is increasingly interested in the human person as a unified whole. The gospel we proclaim must speak to human beings in their entirety. This does not mean merely placing more emphasis on emotion or the affective aspects of life alongside the rational. Rather, it involves integrating the emotional-affective, as well as the bodily-sensual, with the intellectual-rational within one human person.[339]

In conclusion, we see that the evangelical church has allowed the modern context in which it has lived to influence the gospel, giving us a method of salvation that in many cases falls short of the biblical standard. In our attempt to rediscover a proper approach to conversion we can learn from the Postmodern context around

---

[338] T. Yates, *Christian Mission in the Twentieth Century* (Cambridge Universtiy Press, 1994).

[339] "Evangelism involves process and event." See James Emery White, Stanley J. Grenz, *Primer on Postmodernism* (Grand Rapids, Michigan: Eerdmans, 1996), 63; D.A Carson, *The Gagging of God* (Grand Rapids, Michigan: Zondervan, 1996), 172.

us. Conversion is not necessarily "raising your hand", "ticking the check-box on your communication card", or "walking the aisle in an altar call". It is the emergence of a new mode of life as we assume the Christian story, integrate into the Christian community, and learn its language.

A Process View of Conversion and Discipleship

Postmodernists see life as a journey. Every individual, they believe, has a different path to travel. This places them at odds with much of the evangelical tradition, which has tended to emphasize the momentary nature of conversion, and has sought for a universal approach to discipleship.[340] More than a few evangelical authors have sought to break down the concepts of conversion and discipleship into simple steps, in an attempt to design a strategy that could be duplicated regardless of personality and context.

Postmodernists react strongly to such an attempt at universalizing. They are quick to point out that this overlooks the uniqueness of every individual. They believe every person is different and has a unique path to travel. No journey is quite the same, and no one person should seek to make his or her journey the norm for everyone else's journey.

This view of life as a journey, or a process, finds an echo in Scripture. When Jesus told his disciples to make disciples of all nations and to teach them everything he had commanded, no doubt he was talking about more than a one-time experience. Many evangelicals have emphasized the importance of conversion so much that they have lost sight of the importance of the subsequent process of spiritual growth.

---

[340] This is not to say that conversion cannot be momentary, but it does say that conversion is a process, or a sequence of steps. It includes the weakening of the old worldview, the willingness to adopt a new one, and finally the conviction of that new worldview. While it is possible for this process to be completed rapidly, chances are higher it will take an amount of time.

Moreover, we have come to see salvation as a one-moment event rather than a process. But conversion is probably best described as both.[341] "Twentieth century Americans like me", writes Brian McLaren, "were taught to focus on an instant salvation, a decision-oriented regeneration, conversion event." McLaren recommends that we see conversion as a process too. "...birth is the culmination of a long process, and is the commencement of another long process, and in and of itself constitutes a process (and a laborious one at that)."[342] He warns that rushed decisions...tend to be harmful. He recommends that we allow people the time to turn to Christ. In a complicated world like ours, people need time. They may gradually adopt the Christian worldview, enter the Christian community, and learn the Christian language if allowed space.

Bold Apologetics

Much can be said about our apologetic. There is an odd tension between our faith and the Postmodern world. On the one side, we believe in the absolute truthfulness of our claim. We believe the gospel to be universally true. Yet we often find that mere proclamation does not quite have the level of effectiveness we might like. People don't come to Christ because we proclaim that our message is absolutely true. Our claim of absolute truthfulness is surrounded by much competition from radically different belief-systems with the same claim. In such an environment the claim of the absolute truthfulness of the gospel not only serves to make our message uninteresting; it will actually serve to relegate Christians to the fringes of society as irrelevant fundamentalists.

McLaren relates to an occasion he had to address professionals from Communist China about the existence of God.

---

[341] "Evangelism in a Postmodern World," in *The Challenge of Postmodernism - An Evangelical Engagement*, ed., David S. Dockery (Wheaton, Illinois: BridgePoint, 1995), 368-9.

[342] McLaren, 84.

Rather than argue for the existence of God, I felt I should take a different approach. I titled my lecture, "How to think about the existence of God." Instead of arguing for the existence of God, I presented a series of questions one would naturally need to consider in the search for God...I tried to be objective and give each option a fair hearing, and then I explained which answers I had chosen in my own life...I also shared a personal story of how my faith had helped me deal with a difficult experience when my son was diagnosed with leukemia. I told them I hoped these thoughts had been helpful and then opened the floor for questions.

A distinguished gentleman stood, with Asian respect, to ask his questions. "Sir, I do not have a question, but I wish to thank you on behalf of all of us. You have helped us a great deal. Instead of telling us what to believe, you have told us how to believe, and this is very good for us.

Then a woman stood and said, "Yes, I agree with my colleague. You see, in my country whenever anyone tells you what to believe, we know he is lying. The harder he pushes, the more we disbelieve him."[343]

Therefore, we must recognize that our faith ultimately is a story that must be accepted in faith.

To many evangelicals the notion of recognizing that the gospel is ultimately a story that needs to be accepted in faith, sounds dangerously like relativism. To many it sounds like surrender to the secular worldview they have tried so hard to combat. The opposite is true. Recognizing that the gospel, the whole biblical message for that matter, is a story that needs to be accepted in faith is not a capitulation at all. It is merely recognition of the obvious. Of course, the gospel needs to be accepted in faith ~ never was it any different. And by the same token, it goes without saying that we believe in the truthfulness of our gospel. It is implicit in what we

---

[343] McLaren, 72.

say; of course, we believe in the truthfulness of the story we proclaim. It almost goes without saying. The assertion that we believe in the gospel does not come as a surprise to Postmodern people. Of course, we do. Just like Muslims believe their worldview, and the Buddhists theirs, and the Marxists theirs. The assertion that we believe in what we proclaim will not come as a surprise to anyone, but neither will it cause anyone to feel like they too should believe like we do.

No, we need to recognize that our faith is a story, but we believe in that story with an unshakable conviction. We are committed to our story, and we believe and proclaim it boldly. The Christian, like the scientist, should commit himself to a view of reality and its further disclosure "with universal intent" (Polanyi's phrase).[344] This means that while on the one side we understand that our faith is "one story among many stories" at the same time we do not back away from our story as being a metanarrative: a story that gives meaning, significance and order to reality, which in fact is worthy of consideration. Not just because of its meaning-giving function, but even more so because it is true. While we realize that people believe many things, we in fact do believe in the existence of a personal God who has come to seek and save the lost. Our humility in understanding that there are many conflicting truth-claims in the world should not mean that we become less convinced of what we believe, or set it forth any less boldly.

> If we are going to speak to our generation so that we are heard, we must speak as men and women who understand that the world is fragmented and divided, who are honest in facing up to this fact, and who offer real answers and a real solution for this. We must present a gospel that speaks to all of life, not just the "spiritual part," and that is relevant to the concerns Busters feel about interpersonal relationships, the environment, racial and class prejudice, and ethnic diversity. In short, we must

---

[344] T. Yates, *Christian Mission in the Twentieth Century* (Cambridge University Press, 1994).

proclaim the gospel of Ephesians 1, the message of Paul, the good news about Jesus Christ, who is the one focal point for cosmic reintegration and the One worshiped by a new, reconciled community characterized by faith, hope, and love.[345]

A Proclamation and Life-Style of Hope

The hopelessness of Generation X has been well-documented. Sociologically speaking, it is the result of the breakdown of family and community, the increasing complexity of everyday life, and a worldview that offers no solace. Yet the gospel is the answer to the longings of the Postmodern generation.[346] Todd Hahn and David Verhaagen write in their aptly-named book *Reckless Hope:*

> We all live in a seemingly hopeless world, a world that is out of control, filled with violence and hatred and injustice. Yet those of us who know Jesus have a hope that transcends this temporary despair. God can be trusted to be good and to come through for us. We do have a hope that does not disappoint us.[347]

Servant Evangelism

In the Modernist era, evangelicals put great trust in proclamation-evangelism as the *modus operandi* to bring people to Christ. This is understandable if we realize that Modernism places great trust in language as a means of communication, and in its ability to objectively communicate truth. But in the Postmodern era, such trust is radically displaced by skepticism. Postmodernism follows a line of thought that originated with Nietzsche, and that sees all claims to truth largely as devices which serve to legitimate power-interests. "Disguise covers everything. Hence, a culture of

---

[345] Todd Hahn and David Verhaagen, *Reckless Hope - Understanding and. Reaching Baby-Busters* (Grand Rapids, Michigan: Baker Book House, 1996), 75.

[346] Grenz, 174.

[347] Hahn and Verhaagen, 97.

distrust and suspicion emerges."[348] Inspired by such thinking, people in the Postmodern era will be characterized by a great amount of skepticism towards those who preach at them. The listener is always thinking "What are you trying to sell me?"[349]

One possible form of evangelism that bypasses this whole question is "servant evangelism". Instead of assuming the role of "the teacher", or "the salesman", the Christian assumes the role of the servant. By doing so he or she will be perceived in Postmodern eyes as being consistent with Christ's person and message.

Thiselton, inspired by Bonhoeffer, writes:

> Authentic Christian faith lies in identification with the Christ who neither sought power by manipulation, nor was "weak" in the sense of being bland, conformist, or world-denying, He was "the man for others...Faith does not use God, either as a pretext for legitimizing one's wishes, or to explain gaps in certain intellectual problems. Biblical Christianity is controlled by the model not of religiosity, but of the Christ who goes to the cross 'for the other".[350]

For some reason humility seems to make sense to everyone except for veteran churchgoers, writes Steve Sjogren, author of the book *Servant Evangelism*. And yet it is normal for Christians to serve those outside the Church.[351] Aware of how tired people are of just another attempted pitch for some party or group, and how

---

[348] Anthony C. Thiselton, *Interpreting God and the Postmodern Self* (Grand Rapids Michigan: Eerdrnans, 1995), 12.

[349] Which is of course the commercial or contemporary equivalent to Nietzsche's question: How is the communicator trying to establish power over his audience?

[350] Op. Cit., 23.

[351] Steve Sjogren, *Conspiracy of Kindness - A Refreshing New Approach to Sharing the Love of Jesus with Others* (Ann Arbor, Michiogan: Servant Publications, 1993), 19. Sjogren defines 'Servant Evangelism' as "Demonstrating the kindness of God by offering some act of humble service with no strings attached" (p. 17). Examples are a free car-wash, free handy-man labor, and giving out free popsicles. Sjogren does not see servant evangelism as the tool or strategy of the future, but simply as one method among many (pp. 21-22).

confused they are from the many worldviews that seem to contradict each other, yet all clamor for attention, Sjogren suggests an alternative approach to evangelism that has worked very well for him.[352] He writes that servant evangelism gives people a picture of God, in that the service is provided free, for no other reason than the desire to demonstrate God's love.

Unchurched people have many ideas about Christians that are not positive. Sjogren mentions "church lady", a popular character on *Saturday Night Live*, and demonstrates that the reason American people find her funny is because she portrays the superiority that so many people sense from Christians so well.[353] The Gospel only actually becomes good news when it is incarnated in the lives of those who claim to be Christ's followers. Unchurched people need to see us demonstrate an attitude of humility, not superiority; they need to see love, and not pride or smugness. Such demonstration is a necessary part of our apologetic. The proper form of apologetics, writes Lesslie Newbigin, "is the preaching of the gospel itself and the demonstration - which is not merely or primarily a matter of words - that it does provide the best foundation for a way of grasping and dealing with the mystery of our existence in this universe."[354]

Local Outreach

A catch phrase for Postmodern people is "think globally, act locally." Well aware that the world is a large and complex place, Postmodern people want to know that they are making an impact

---

[352] Steve Sjogren is the founding pastor of Vineyard Community Church in Cincinnati, Ohio, which he started with a group of five that ultimately grew under his leadership to a weekend attendance of over 6,000. In the course of that journey, Steve mentored numerous church planters who launched likeminded churches in the Ohio Valley. Steve is considered by many in the church world to be the father of servant evangelism - the notion that "the kindness of God brings us to repentance" (Rom. 2: 4).

[353] Sjogren, 28-29.

[354] Lesslie Newbigin, *Proper Confidence: Faith, Doubt and Certainty in Christian Discipleship* (Grand Rapids Michigan: Eerdmans, 1995), and quoted in Stafford, 24.

in their local communities.[355] While there is a fascination with far-away places, and an ever-present desire to learn more about them, Postmodern people do not consider organizations that are not effective on the local level credible. They want to see you practice what you preach, see how what you practice makes a difference, and see if what you do is indeed a blessing.

There is perhaps much in these last chapters that is challenging to the evangelical mind. The issues raised challenge the way many evangelicals have done ministry for the last number of decades. They propose alternatives that seem more viable in the Postmodern context. But as viable as they may be, they are not familiar to us. For some evangelicals, this is like the liberal theology they have grown to dislike. Naturally, they are concerned. What will happen to their view of the Scriptures, or their view of truth? Is their orthodoxy in danger? And yet, there is a world "out there" that is becoming increasingly Postmodern. In large parts of it, Postmodernism became the dominant cultural force some time ago. At the same time the way we have sought to reach people with the gospel is not yielding the results, we desire. By all accounts, we are not quite as successful in reaching Postmodern people as we would like to be. This situation should lead us to reconsider what we do and how we do it.

> A saying among management experts today is, "Your system is perfectly designed to yield the results you are getting." This is a profound, though, painful truth, which must be respected by all who have an interest in Christian spiritual formation, whether for themselves as individuals or for groups or institution.[356]

Perhaps that change is never comfortable. Understandably it is very difficult for those who have fought so hard against the evils of Modernism, to now see that the nature of the fight has changed and that yesterday's foes are becoming today's allies. Our defenses

---

[355] Nash, 104.

[356] Dallas Willard, *The Divine Conspiracy* (San Francisco, CA: Harper San Francisco, 1998), 58.

against Modernism have become unhelpful in our attempts to evangelize Postmodern people. Change is necessary, and new avenues and possibilities must be explored.

There are many examples of Postmodern ministry in new expressions of the church such as the Emergent and Missional movements. Some of what is being done are admirable, and some of what is being done is questionable. What is good should be affirmed and what is bad should be avoided.

Given the benefit of hindsight, it is important to look back at these experimental phenomena and try to evaluate what began to emerge in the latter decades of the twentieth-century. There has been a certain trajectory which ought to be measured. When it comes to measuring anything, be it time, distance, volume, capacity, etc., a standard is needed. In spiritual matters the only true standard is Scripture, so all forms of church practice are subject to measurement by its principles and precepts.

Chapter 10 Observations and Concerns

There is now a movement "within" the church that is disillusioned with the existing model and methods of traditional church practice. I am not just referring to a restless few who dislike conservative mainstream denominational churches. I am not just referring to people who want to move away from church buildings with pews, elevated pulpits and stained-glass windows. The same attitude is adopted with regard to churches with more modern buildings and more contemporary styles of worship. I am referring to what is known as the missional church.

What is the church? What is its nature and purpose? What is its role in this world? What is its relationship to the wider community? What are its sacred and secular responsibilities? What is a Christian? What is the gospel? What is mission? What is evangelism? In our eagerness to engage with contemporary culture these questions tend to be neglected. But they come into focus if we try to unite in inter-church collaboration on evangelism. Without broad consensus, any such endeavor will be problematic. But we also need a clear understanding of the answers to these questions within our own church community.

Church communities are being drawn into the vortex of unhelpful and unhealthy alliances ostensibly for the sake of evangelism and engagement. These problematic partnerships lead to confusion and compromise. I am concerned that people with evangelistic antennae are picking up this signal on their radar and embarking on a route to nowhere. We need to rethink the mission paradigm in the light of emerging challenges. We need to keep mission central to church life. We need to be in tune with the rhythm of God's heartbeat. But we need biblical perspectives on mission theology as a prerequisite to identifying the way forward. Why? Because there are new directions in mission and it is important to examine these new departures. I want to take the missional church (the most significant new trend in evangelism and engagement) as a case study and offer a critique of this emerging phenomenon by asking whether it is a menace or catalyst.

The important question to be addressed is whether or not God is at work in this recent phenomenon. Some will say it's the new reality and we better get on board before the ship leaves shore. We cannot simply endorse something just because it is a reality; we must be more discerning. For this, we will need some criteria for evaluating a work of the Holy Spirit.

Is the missional church a menace? Some perceive it as a threat to the welfare of the church. Is it a dangerous development? It seems (as a father of three) that new life has a nuisance element to it in as much as it disrupts life as it has been heretofore. But new life is to be welcomed, cherished and guided. Certainly the missional church is a catalyst insofar as it is precipitating change. The question I want to address is: "Is this change a good thing?" It is a development which has implications not only for missiology but also for Christology and ecclesiology.

The "attractional" church is understood as a church with a building that is used for regular worship services, prayer meetings, Bible studies, Sunday school, youth group meetings and a host of other programs and activities. It is argued (by missional church advocates) that in this postmodern culture the "attractional" church is outmoded. It has been so named because of the idea that the church's missional stance is futile. They see it as ineffective in connecting with contemporary culture because it is based on the hope that people will be attracted to our pews by our preaching and programs. It might be likened to lighthouses which were once manned and useful but have become irrelevant in a world where seafarers have sophisticated navigation technology based on global positioning systems.

The new movement in evangelism and engagement advocates what it calls "incarnational" communities. These communities are essentially mission-focused, seeker-centered alternatives to the attractional church model. The locus of mission is re-centered so that instead of expecting un-churched people to come to us we are exhorted to go to them. Clearly there is much merit in taking such an approach. The exponents of this new way would advocate launching lifeboats rather than building lighthouses as a mission strategy.

So what? At first glance, it might sound like nothing more than a different way of fishing for souls. But it is not. This is not a movement that advocates a different way of doing church or merely an attempt to put mission at the center of church life. If we stay with the nautical analogy for a moment they would say that doing church differently is like re-arranging the deck chairs on the Titanic. So they see existing attractional church models (our churches) as doomed structures, and they are sounding the bell to abandon ship. But are they entering uncharted waters in crafts that will not withstand the fury of the raging seas?

There is some concern that some people in this new movement do not have the theological competence to pilot these flimsy vessels. But some of its leaders have advanced theological training and are directors of global networks and are quite organized in their approach to the dissemination of this new thinking through publication, consultation and training. One has to admire the energy of these radical activists. We can be defensive and rigid and reject this new order, but that would be as unwise as unquestioningly embracing it. What is needed is an honest, open-minded critique of this movement rather than a gut-feeling response rooted in a predisposed antipathy to anything perceived as novel or trendy.

Has the attractional church passed its "best before" date? According to the leading exponents of the missional movement it is time to shut our doors and walk away before the sun sets on the institutionalized church form.

God can and does work in surprising ways and unexpected places. The evangelical community is primarily conservative and tends to keep its distance from anything that it perceives as problematic and messy. But what is perceived as a problem may be an opportunity to provide leadership and discipleship. We do need to think about the dynamics of our relationship with the missional church.

According to missional church literature this movement is seeing people being converted, lives being changed, a searching of the Scriptures and evidence of a new love for God and one another. Some will say that surely this is to be welcomed and that God does not need our permission to act in unexpected ways. The argument might be offered that, sadly, the Christian establishment is often dragged reluctantly into acknowledging God's work outside its own restricted circles.

Once Upon a Time

I once read a story about a lifeboat station on the Eastern Coast of the United States.

It had begun when some of the locals with sailing experience became concerned about the number of ships that got into trouble in their waters. So they clubbed together and bought a lifeboat. Then they built a boathouse to keep it in. Over the years, many lives were saved and there were countless instances of remarkable bravery. Often when the men were out on a rescue, the women would gather at the boathouse, comforting one another as they waited anxiously for news of their husbands. They discovered they worried less if they kept busy, so they put up curtains on the boathouse windows and generally smartened the place up. They persuaded their husbands (when not out on rescues) to put in a little kitchen and some comfortable chairs. Over the years, the boathouse became a much more comfortable place to wait. In fact it became so comfortable that the men and their wives used to meet there sometimes when there was no rescuing to be done. Sometimes they brought friends who had never been out in a lifeboat in their lives. Some of the friends moored their yachts nearby. Gradually the character of the lifeboat station changed. One day there was a furious storm and a ship got into trouble just a little way along the coast. The people were all very concerned but no one went out to help. Why? The lifeboat station had become a yacht club.[357]

Many people are now saying that our churches have ceased to be rescue stations for the lost and have become comfortable clubs for the saved.

In fairness to the missional church, which is seeking to create incarnational communities, it must be said that they are well-meaning, sincere, hardworking, and dedicated to achieving their goals. They rightly understand that there is a problem concerning reaching the un-churched. They correctly understand that dwindling church attendance and declining numbers of church adherents is a worrying trend. However, because they are evangelists, they think that everything in the church should center on evangelism.

I think all believers would want to place huge importance on evangelism but in a balanced way. People with evangelistic antennae have a tendency to develop tunnel vision. The church needs people with these gifts but some blinkered individuals who do not have a panoramic view of the church think that evangelism is all that really matters. I have no doubt that many zealous but theologically naïve individuals are attracted to emerging situations. But I believe the more discerning churches will pick and mix the best and most innovative approaches and this is to be encouraged.

What Is Church?

When it comes to understanding the missional church (which is essentially a Postmodern phenomenon) it is important to examine the biblical basis for Christian community. We all agree that a church is not a building in which Christians meet for worship. Rather the local church consists of a fellowship of believers who gather to worship God. If we do not understand the biblical basis for Christian community we will be terribly confused about the

---

[357] Gary Benfold, "So that I can rebuild it", *Evangelical Magazine of Wales*, May/June, 2004.

nature of true fellowship. An obvious concern about new directions in evangelism and engagement, which needs to be addressed, is that "fellowship" with unbelievers is more a kind of camaraderie, which does not constitute true unity of the Holy Spirit.

Many church leaders will agree with the missional church's *diagnosis* concerning the condition of the attractional church in the twenty-first century. But it is their *prognosis* and *prescription* that causes some concern. It is important for every generation to find ways of communicating the gospel to its culture but there is a danger that in seeking to be relevant we cross a line that ought not to be crossed.

Seeker-Centered or Seeker-Sensitive?

An occupational hazard for evangelists and church planters is that they become seeker-centered (as distinct from seeker-sensitive) and cross the line between contextualization and syncretism. Contextualization is about finding ways of explaining and exhibiting the gospel that can be understood within a particular cultural context, without compromising the integrity of the message or the messenger. Syncretism occurs when the desire to be relevant transcends all other motives and both message and messenger become integrated into the prevailing cultural context.[358] Syncretism occurs when Christians adapt, either consciously or unconsciously, to the prevailing worldview. It is the reshaping of Christian beliefs and practices so that they reflect those of the dominant culture. In this process, Christianity loses it distinctiveness.[359] Syncretism is frequently birthed from a yearning

---

[358] The publisher, Christian Publishing House, would recommend that the reader consider the following article,

Contextualization, Seeker-Movement, or Seeker Sensitive Methods of Evangelism =Nine Parts World to One Part Christian

http://www.christianpublishers.org/you-are-no-part-of-the-world

[359] Gailyn Van Rheenen, "Modern and Postmodern Syncretism in Theology and Missions", *The Holy Spirit and Mission Dynamics*, ed. C. Douglas McConnell (Pasadena: Wm. Carey, 1997), 173.

to make the gospel appear relevant. The church attempts to make its message attractive to outsiders and as these adaptations become regularly assimilated they form an integral part of the church's life. When significant changes in worldview take place the Christian community, swept along by the ebb and flow of cultural currents, begins to lose her moorings.[360]

There has been a significant paradigm shift best summarized by the word "Postmodernism," as discussed in the previous chapters. Some church people are wondering if it will come into the church. The reality is that it is well embedded in the church. Many churches have gone beyond the process of contextualizing the gospel in Western culture and have married themselves to these core values of society. One writer cautions:

> While Christian witness must be savvy concerning the realities of the Postmodern condition in order to make the historic Christian message understandable and pertinent to denizens of the contemporary world, this does not mean that we should become postmodernists in the process.[361]

Radical Developments

There are many radical developments in how the church is practiced today. We are going to see much more of this kind of thoroughgoing recalibration in the next decades. The orientation toward missional and incarnational communities is not merely a rediscovery of the values and vision of the ancient faith communities found in the book of Acts. We must be careful not to disregard centuries of subsequent church history (including the Reformation) as if they are entirely irrelevant. That would be like throwing the baby out with the bathwater, and that is a calamitous thing to do. Has our failure to address mission in a holistic way

---

[360] Ibid.

[361] Douglas Groothuis, "Facing the Challenge of Postmodernism", *To Everyone and Answer: A Case for the Christian Worldview*, Francis Beckwith, William Lane Craig and J. P. Moreland eds. (Downers Grove, Illinois: IVP, 2004), 253.

partly contributed to new departures in evangelism and engagement?[362]

The missional church is not a counter-cultural movement; it is, in fact, the opposite. Indeed, they react to the consumerist, materialistic and therapeutic values of modernist churches that have developed too cozy a relationship with the prevailing cultural norms. There is a real danger that they will lose their distinct identity as Christians.

The missional church contends that traditional Christian identity is perceived as unattractive to Postmodern seekers. It charges the church with creating self-serving institutions that are not connecting with community. It would say that the attractional church has merely created holy huddles which are no-go zones for unbelievers who do not feel they belong to these "clubs". They say that we have retrenched into our private enclaves. The accusation that we live a kind of neo-monastic existence is not entirely untrue.

Missional church people integrate themselves into various communities and sub-cultures and intentionally conceal their spiritual identities until they have built what they call, "meaningful relationships". I feel there is something inappropriate and dishonest in this kind of subterfuge. I think Christians are called to be conspicuous in this world, not chameleons who adapt to the surrounding environment. We should not be disingenuous about our intentions. Christians are to be *in* the world but not *of* the world. D. L. Moody said, "The ship is meant to be in the water but God help her when the water gets into the ship." It is an obvious truth, which states an important principle of Christian living.

The missional church claims to be involved in creating places of inclusive belonging where God's kingdom can be experienced. This sounds good until what that actually means is spelled out. Certainly, Christians should be creating places of welcome but we

---

[362] I have witnessed holistic models of mission working well in India and Eastern Europe but I acknowledge the dangers inherent in this model whereby the gospel message of salvation can become subordinate to material concerns.

should not adopt an "end-justifies-the–means" approach to winning souls. The church is the bride of Christ and should remain pure and uncompromised.

Some new directions in evangelism and engagement are manifestations of a myopic movement, which appeals to the disaffected and trend-orientated. Any critique of their motives and methods is viewed with suspicion and deemed to be judgmental. They dismiss people who present a different theological perspective as those who, "know too much, talk too much and judge too much."[363] This is both unfair and unhelpful.

The missional church criticism of the attractional church is rooted in the observation that there are so few conversions. They say churches are, "musty, fussy, clubby, judgmental, mean, punishing, ungenerous..."[364] It is an unfair generalization to have the faithful and fervent work of so many pastors, elders, deacons and church members denigrated in this way. Yet we must examine ourselves to see if there is an element of truth in this.

Schismatic Squabble

Differences about how evangelism and engagement are to be conducted have the potential to give rise to schismatic squabbles. I don't want to contribute to polemical "debate" but new directions have potentially dangerous undercurrents, and I think it would be negligent not to flag this. Our desire to engage with Postmodern culture must have safeguards against being ensnared by it. Otherwise, many who start out meaning well might end up watching Oprah, Larry King or Dr. Phil for spiritual guidance.

What are we to make of pastors leaving churches to become baristas and barmen in the belief that in so doing they will be more

---

[363] Hugh Halter and Matt Smay, *The Tangible Kingdom*, (San Francisco: CA, Jossey-Bass, 2008), xxii

[364] Hugh Halter and Matt Smay, *The Tangible Kingdom* (San Francisco: CA, Jossey-Bass, 2008), 11.

effective witnesses for Christ? I suggest that people who do this were never ideally suited to pastoral ministry. Rather they were church planters and evangelists. I wish them well but hope their new mission outpost situations will stay connected to local church communities.

For the missional church connecting with Postmodern sojourners is paramount. They establish communities which permit anybody, irrespective of belief or behavior, to belong. It appears to have a disregard for doctrine and tradition and argues that we should set aside our apologetics and theology and include those outside the Kingdom.

Church communities must be places of benevolence and blessing. We must extend a warm and genuine welcome to all. However, the theological and biblical reality is that one does not *belong* to Christ until and unless one has repented of one's sin and confessed Christ as Savior. We should not pretend that people belong when in fact they do not. That would be deceptive and unwise. It is like allowing people to come to our homes and dine with us. We can have a great deal of interaction but they are not members of our family.

Some new directions in mission tend to have an end justifies– the means approach to involving non-believers in church ministries. This has resulted in incidents such as stoned and drunk musicians playing at their gatherings and the unconverted teaching Bible stories to children. Boundaries are blurred, and nobody in their communities is bothered by this.

Because society has lost interest in "organized Christendom," there is a desire to offer it a radical alternative. An important question, therefore, is whether or not this alternative is authentic to the ideals of Scripture.

The missional church seems to have lost confidence in the efficacy of preaching to accomplish God's purposes. Maybe they have been exposed to poor models of preaching and sadly, there is much of that about. I believe that preaching Christ in a postmodern culture is not only feasible but imperative. The missional church argues that people won't change by listening to preaching. I wonder why Jesus preached. Jesus was first and foremost a preacher. The Nazareth Manifesto identifies preaching as central to his ministry.[365] If we want to be models of Christ we cannot dismiss preaching. Even by their own admission the missional church says that "Christology determines missiology, and missiology determines ecclesiology."[366] The whole notion of church is being systematically deconstructed and radically redefined in contemporary Postmodern culture.

To Boldly Go Where No Man Has Gone Before

The missional desire to spend time with the un-churched is admirable. They see themselves as pioneers who are taking risks in going, "where no man has gone before". For them the fulfillment of the Great Commission to "go" is not merely about outreach evangelism programs, rather it is about living among and belonging. But we must love the found as well as the lost. To what extent (if any) have we contributed to the sense of disaffection which is giving rise to this movement by inserting extra-biblical proscriptions, written and unwritten, (about issues like alcohol, smoking, styles of dress, etc.) as conditions of membership in constitutions and codes of conduct.

It is difficult to get the balance right between being a community which confronts the godless values of the cultural norms and being an inclusive community. The missional church is calling for a revolution in inclusive community in which the masses will want to participate. The distaste for present forms of church is evident in the words of Hugh Halter, "The typical message has been to be good, stop sinning, go to church, and wait for God to

---

[365] Luke 4:18-19

[366] Michael Frost and Alan Hirsch, *The Shaping of Things to Come*, (Massachusetts: USA, Hendrickson, 2003 and Australia: Strand Publishing), 16.

come back. Yuck. It's too simple."[367] Surely it is right to stop sinning. Sin is grievously offensive to God and to cease sinning is an indication that the person has newness of life. This is what God wants and expects of converts. Is it not right to go to a place where like-minded people assemble to worship God as a community of believers? Did not the early church have an eschatological hope that radically altered how it lived?

The missional church believes that through benevolent action in the community spiritual dialogue will ensue and so they openly admit that they would prefer do something useful (like picking up litter in the community) on Sunday morning instead of going to church. They will randomly cancel their gatherings so that they can do something alternative to "worship". But the kingdom of God is not about winning the "Tidy Towns" competition! Some churches have involved their youth in making a positive contribution to the community by clearing up litter. This kind of activity can be very positive and can open doors of opportunity to conversations about how our faith motivates us to do good deeds. The problem is in conducting such benevolent acts as *alternatives* to church worship services. The missional church does not seem to care much if people attend their Sabbath gatherings. They encourage people to spend their Sunday mornings being with sojourners. Perhaps the missional church is attractive because one does not have to forsake much or believe much in order to belong to it.

The missional church talks about *apprenticing* disciples as more authentic than *cognitive* discipleship. However, Jesus taught his disciples for three years and the Great Commission instructs us to "teach" all that Christ has taught. This is clearly part of the discipleship process. Maybe the discipleship process is best done through supervised hands-on experience supplemented with teaching.

---

[367] Hugh Halter and Matt Smay, *The Tangible* Kingdom (Massachusetts: USA, Hendrickson, 2003 and Australia: Strand Publishing) 74.

In his trenchant analysis of the cultural corruption, weakening the church's thought and witness, David Wells argues that evangelicals have blurred the distinctions between Christ and culture, and have largely abandoned their traditional emphasis on divine transcendence in favor of an emphasis on divine immanence. In doing so, they have produced a faith in God that is of little consequence to those who believe. He says, "There is a profound sense in which the church has to be 'otherworldly.'"[368]

Nobody is saying that everything in existing structures and the prevailing *modus operandi* is sacrosanct. We must be open to the idea of reviewing our structures to see if they hinder or help our goals. But all of this must be done in the light of Scripture. In this new movement church becomes a discovery zone for participating sojourners where the desire to be relevant leads to convictions being diluted. We must be careful about how we proceed so that what is harmful can be rejected and what is helpful can be retained as we seek to advance in evangelism and engagement.

Evaluating Criteria

Are there any criteria that can be used to evaluate contemporary approaches to mission? What is a genuine work of the Holy Spirit? One would certainly hesitate to make unfair accusations or derive inappropriate conclusions about any activity which might be authentic. John MacArthur has presented material condensed, adapted and excerpted from Jonathan Edwards's, "The Distinguishing Marks of a Work of the Spirit of God."[369] This MacArthur/Edwards article identifies five distinguishing characteristics of the Holy Spirit's work, based on an analysis of 1 John 4:1-8. These are helpful in determining whether or not emerging trends are a true work of God. MacArthur says that a genuine work of the Holy Spirit exalts the true Christ, opposes

---

[368] David F. Wells, *God in the Wasteland: The Reality of Truth in a World of Fading Dreams* (Wm. B. Eerdmans, Grand Rapids: Michigan, and Inter-Varsity Press, Leicester: England, 1994) 41.

[369] 'A True Work of the Spirit', © John MacArthur, Jr, 'Grace to You' See also: http://www.biblebb.com/files/edwards/je-marksofhs.htm

Satan's interests, points people to the Scriptures, elevates truth and results in love for God and others. Let us examine the new phenomenon in the light of this standard.

First, we must ask if the missional church upholds a Scriptural view of Christ. Clearly, the doctrine of the incarnation must be affirmed. The missional church subscribes to this truth in asserting that Jesus is the Son of God.[370] This community of believers (and I think that is, generally, what they are) genuinely desires to lead people to Christ. Christ is revered (perhaps sentimentally) in this new movement.

Nevertheless, there is something imaginary about the Christ they extol. I have already asserted that Jesus was a preacher. The missional church makes a distinction between "Galilean" Christians and "Jerusalem" Christians. The Galilean Christians are those who interpret the Bible through the life of Jesus. The Jerusalem Christians are more doctrinal. This bias toward the Galilean way is quite subjective. They see Jerusalem people as idolaters of the Bible who have overly intellectualized spirituality. Thus Postmodern missional people have reduced the Bible to the gospels and argue that if we only had the gospels Christianity would look very different today. But we have the entire canon of Scripture because God wanted to reveal more than what is disclosed in the Gospels. Their tendency to ignore, reject or devalue any Scripture that is not directly spoken by Jesus is potentially heretical.

Second, a distinguishing mark of a work of the Spirit of God is that it will oppose Satan's interests. Satan desires that people remain in a sinful condition and succumb to the lusts of the flesh. The missional church is not entirely indifferent to sinfulness, but its attitude to sin is lax. I am not saying they are dens of iniquity. They claim to create an environment in which the conscience can become sensitive to the truth in relation to sin. But in the absence

---

[370] As far as I am aware they believe in the sinless life, substitutionary death/atonement, resurrection, ascension, intercessory role, divinity, trinity and second coming of Christ.

of preaching about the dreadfulness of sin they have created an environment which is casual about sin.

A third mark that distinguishes a work of the Spirit of God is that it points people to the Scriptures. The missional church does not induce a high a regard for the whole counsel of God. As already mentioned, they tend to be red-letter people rather than biblical people.[371] In other words, they put a higher value on the words of Christ than on the words of other authors of Scripture. This distorts revelation.

The fourth feature of a work of the Spirit of God is that it elevates truth. Indeed, the missional church makes people more aware of the central gospel truths. They may be effective in leading people to faith but fall short of leading them to maturity in Christ.

The fifth and final mark that distinguishes a work of the Spirit of God is that it results in love for God and others. The missional church loves the lost and it is to be highly commended for this. They profess to love God, and I don't doubt their sincerity in this regard. Nevertheless, the God they profess to love is eviscerated of much of the divine nature as a sin-loathing God.

The missional church is not heretical but it is a movement, which has potentially harmful effects. Nevertheless, in spite of reservations about and objections to its "unorthodox" irregularities and potential hazards it cannot be dismissed as a work of Satan. Must it, therefore, be embraced as a work of the Holy Spirit? From past experience (consider the history of revival movements) it is clear that the Spirit of God can work even in the midst of much that might be deemed "problematic."

We should be very reluctant, therefore, to condemn a work in which the Holy Spirit might be involved and we should have a similar sense of hesitancy about contributing to the polarization of differing Christian communities. But we must test the spirits and

---

[371] In many Bibles the words of Jesus are printed in red ink.

where we find deficiencies and dangers we must be diligent in alerting others to the potential pitfalls.

The Way Forward

One's theology shapes One's ideas about mission. Much has been written in recent years about mission, which focuses on methodological approaches to engaging contemporary culture. Many of these works boldly propose new ways of engaging with contemporary culture. We must be concerned about keeping mission central to church life and identifying a way forward in the labyrinthine complexity of Postmodern society.

The trendy literature suggests that the "attractional" model of the church of Christendom is outmoded. It is an influential body of work, which contends that what is needed now is a "missional" and "incarnational" Christian church. However, these works tend to be primarily focused on how to engage in mission rather than putting in place a theological foundation which would underpin the missionary enterprise. What is needed is a biblical perspective on mission theology, which informs and shapes our understanding, approaches and methodologies in facing the unfinished task of, "making disciples of all nations". This will not only safeguard and strengthen mission but will also provide a means of evaluating trends, which seek to influence future directions in mission activity.

Postmodernism presents a new frontier situation. We must have a missionary impulse to bear witness to the gospel. Certainly we must adapt to the new environment but without compromising. In our Postmodern society we live with the tension of seeking ways of contextualizing the gospel without capitulating to culture. As the current cultural context is emerging we are in uncharted waters and navigating our way will require experienced and savvy people at the helm.

Paradigm shift

It is generally acknowledged now that a paradigm shift has taken place (from Modernism to Postmodernism). This "cultural sea change" has contributed to significantly widening the gulf between church and culture.[372] This is not necessarily a bad thing because the Western church has had too cozy a relationship with the prevailing culture. We now have to talk not about "culture" but "cultures" because we live in what might be called a "pluriverse" rather than a "universe". In this kaleidoscopic cultural context we are all influenced by a variety of cultures in diet, dress, art, architecture, music and the media. Secularization, cultural and religious pluralism, globalization, advances in technology have all impacted on the church's role in society. It is not just city center churches that have this *mélange* of cultures but rural churches as well. It is in response to such challenges that new directions and departures in evangelism and engagement have emerged in a Postmodern context.

Navigating this emerging missiological landscape will involve experimenting with approaches to ministry that will challenge present understandings of what it means to be the church today. These challenges are new opportunities to engage in innovative forms of communication and dialogue. Should we consider this taking place in unconventional spaces, often referred to as "the third place"? This would mean inhabiting places outside church buildings that are also inhabited by non-Christians. The missional church thinks in terms of *shared* space rather than *sacred* space. They see the commitment to buildings as an absurd loyalty akin to the captain going down with the sinking ship. In one way they are right ~ buildings should not be consecrated and it is not appropriate to refer to places within such buildings (usually one's with steeples) as "sanctuaries". The apostle clearly spoke on this matter when he addressed the Areopagus, "The God who made the world and everything in it, being Lord of heaven and earth, does not live in temples made by man." Evangelists and theologians must work together like architects and engineers in constructing a new order, which is both attractive and safe.

---

[372] Graham Ward, "Introduction: 'Where We Stand'," in *The Blackwell Companion to Postmodern Theology*, ed. Graham Ward (Oxford and Malden, Mass.: Blackwell Publishers, 2001) xv.

Being Church Today

So, what does it mean to be the church today? It is about participating in a way of life. It means an understanding that we are the gathered community of God's people. We gather around Christ and a body of divinity, indwelt by the Holy Spirit, united as blood brothers. We can create all sorts of artificial communities but the church is an organism, not an organization. It is a living, dynamic and organic entity of the redeemed.

The missional church challenges believers to leave their private enclaves, comfort zones, and infiltrate unorthodox and even profane places. But discernment is needed. Some will reject the call out of hand as an invitation to compromise, which can only result in Christians being contaminated. Others will rush in "where angels fear to tread".

When visiting a city it is helpful to find the map that says, "you are here" accompanied by a big arrow pointing to the spot, or to get your bearings on a smartphone. We can navigate from there. Concerning evangelism and engagement with Postmodern people, there is a sense in which the landscape does not change and the map does not change, but we need to know where we are and re-orientate the map so that we can head in the right direction.

Evangelism is not an elective element of the spiritual life. These new approaches to evangelism and engagement have far-reaching implications because they are not proposing prioritizing mission within existing church structures. It is not about churches giving more time to mission or conducting outreach more often. It is not about preaching more about mission or having more missionaries come and speak in the local church. It is not about more time being given to prayer for mission. It is, rather, a "complete reorientation of the church, a reshaping of its life, a rediscovery of mission as the activity around which everything else is coordinated."[373]

---

[373] Michael Frost, *Encounter with God*: Scripture (Union Bible Reading Notes, July-September, 2010), 45.

Emerging Phenomenon

In the West we are now living in what may be called the post-Christendom era. Many people are no longer interested in what the church has to offer. Paradoxically in Postmodern culture there is a new openness to spirituality. In this situation, where the church, in its present institutionalized form is perceived as irrelevant, growing numbers of Christians are engaging in more innovative missionary activity. However, some of the stories gathered from these emergent church projects give rise to some concern about the future direction of mission. These spirited experiments are primarily motivated by a desire, within the church, to be more relevant to society in the twenty-first century. This relatively new movement is not comprised merely of armchair theorists. Rather this is a radicalized and organized cohort of activists who are effectively disseminating their message, recruiting adherents and replicating missional communities in Western society.

The missional church is a Postmodern expression of the emerging church phenomenon. It deemphasizes what it perceives as "divisive" doctrine by emphasizing the primacy of relationship. This is characteristically postmodern. They also elevate God's (almost indiscriminate) love for mankind over his essential holiness. By raising unity above truth, the missional church creates an atmosphere where peace is the *summum bonum*, that is, the supreme good from which all others are derived.

The missional church is fundamentally rooted in Postmodern culture and this fact may be the cause of its own demise. Philosophies that are driven by culture are inexorably destined to disappear in time. As Os Guinness warned, "He who marries the spirit of the age soon becomes a widower."[374]

The greatest threats to the health of the church are liberalism on the one hand and legalism on the other. The *avant-garde* are

---

[374] Os Guinness, *Dining with the Devil*, (Grand Rapids: Baker, 1993). I have been informed that Google References attributes this remark to W. R. Inge, the famed Dean of St Paul's Cathedral.

the adventurers and innovators who pioneer new approaches and departures. They are more likely to gravitate to liberalism than legalism. The missional church mentality is compatible with this instinct. The rearguard, however, is comprised of those whose instinct is conservative and whose desire is to protect and preserve the status quo and as such, they are more likely to gravitate to legalism. I think we all have a default mode in this regard.

Faith should not be inert and unchanging rather it should be dynamic and vibrant. Our experiences of life must inspire reflection and our interaction with others who hold different views ought to stimulate honest appraisal and reappraisal of our own opinions and positions. Daniel Migliore says:

> ...theology must be critical reflection on the community's faith and practice...not simply a reiteration of what has been or is currently believed and practiced by a community of faith. It is a quest for truth, and that presupposes that the proclamation and practice of the community of faith are always in need of examination and reform...When this responsibility is neglected...the faith of the community is invariably threatened by shallowness, arrogance and ossification.[375]

Those with a risk-taking disposition want to face the white-water rapids in a canoe. Those with a conservative bias would prefer to take a trip in a barge on the canal. It is unlikely that those with a risk-taking disposition and those with a conservative bias will enjoy a journey together. The disposition of the reformers at the time of the Reformation was not conservative. This may be a surprise to those who revere the reformers as establishment heroes. We must cherish a past that is not only connected to the present but also connected to the future.

At the outset I asked if the missional church was a menace or a catalyst. I believe it is both. The words of Mr. Spock might be

---

[375] Daniel L. Migliore, *Faith Seeking Understanding: An Introduction to Christian Theology* (Grand Rapids, Michigan: Eerdmans, 1996), xxi.

applied to the missional church: "It's life, Jim, but not as we know it".

Our theoretical presuppositions about mission and our theological rationale for mission should be determined by the Word of God. We must allow Scripture to speak for itself as the missionary manual rather than impose our views upon it. Eric Wright says:

> Nothing can be more important than to ensure that our missionary presuppositions reflect the principles of Scripture. This will not be true if theology is ignored, because theology brings us face to face with the principles, parameters and priorities that God has revealed.[376]

Mission must be a Christ-centered intentional process of communicating the gospel in word and deed. An informed biblical missional view goes beyond the frequently quoted commissioning passages to a more comprehensive perspective from Genesis to Revelation. Nevertheless the missionary mandate is about living out the Great Commission with the passion of the Great Commandment (to make disciples and love God and neighbor). Christ's followers are to take the gospel to all peoples (nations and ethnic groups) irrespective of class, culture or creed. This demands conviction, commitment and courage in the face of the Postmodern objections of pluralism and the hostility of anti-Christian fundamentalisms.[377] Christians must avoid the pitfall of theological liberalism which perceives evangelism as proselytizing. Christians must also avoid the snare of religious legalism which is nurtured in separatist enclaves.

Our God is a missionary, God. The Bible is a missionary book. The church is a missionary institution. Christ's mandate is a missionary mandate. The Great Commandment (to love) is to be the regulating principle of all mission activity. Postmodern culture

---

[376] Eric E. Wright, *A Practical Theology of Missions: Dispelling the Mystery; Recovering the Passion* (DayOne, UK, 2010) 10.

[377] Such as aggressive atheism and militant secularism.

presents many opportunities for the entrance of the gospel. So each church must find ways of having meaningful interaction with those outside the church. But this must be done without capitulating to the prevailing culture.

The missional church may be over zealous in its approach and naïve in much of its activity, but it has led to some innovative ways of engaging with culture. However, its central problem is its overemphasis on pragmatism. A. W. Tozer identified this issue as far back as 1955 when he said, "Religious pragmatism is running wild among the orthodox. Truth is whatever works. If it gets results it is good."[378]

Eric Wright suggests that "the most pragmatic thing we can do in the long run is to teach what God has revealed, trust his revealed methods and try to apply them in dependence on the Holy Spirit."[379]

Our involvement in the world comes about in a variety of natural and intentional ways. One of the most obvious is in the workplace (though, for pastors this might be a problem because Christians inhabit our world). There are other areas where the Christian may come into contact with the world, such as sports, cultural pursuits, social activities, volunteering, educational programs and local/national politics.

Scripture refers to anyone involved in any form of government as "God's servant" (Romans 13:4). God has ordained the powers that be (Romans 13:10). Clearly, the Christian individual may, in good conscience, be involved in politics. The Old Testament character Daniel walked with God and occupied a senior position in the Babylonian/Persian civil service. Another Old Testament character, Joseph, was directly involved in the government of Egypt. Clearly, therefore, God's people are not forbidden to be involved in society. Some Christians have spearheaded significant

---

[378] A. W. Tozer, *The Root of the Righteous* (Harrisburgh, PA: Christian Publications, 1955), 8.

[379] Eric E. Wright, Op. cit., 10.

social reform, such as William Wilberforce, with the abolition of slavery.

There are many practical and positive ways in which we can let our light shine. Our good deeds give credibility to the gospel message which we proclaim. The Christian is to be concerned for good works as well as good words and this is important in Postmodern society. If we are to model the master we must realize that he was compassionate and went about doing good. – Acts 10:38.

However, there is a difference between humanitarianism and Christian mission. Therefore, we need to ensure that we engage in more than philanthropy. The essential difference is the gospel message of salvation. Christian mission ministers to the soul of humanity and its greatest need: that of a Savior. We must distinguish between the calling of the Christian citizen to engage in social and political action and the mandate of the church. Nevertheless, in certain contexts, the gospel has unavoidable political implications.

Jesus could have gained enormous popularity if he had been willing to respond to the people's political agenda but he resisted. We must do likewise by resisting such temptations and being alert to the danger of being used to further the world's agenda, even when aspects of that agenda are good causes. History abounds with sad examples of the church being hijacked in this way. Para-church organizations which started out with an overtly Christian mission have drifted from their formative ideals and have become virtually secularized.

One of the major dangers facing the Christian church in contemporary culture is religious pluralism. The missionary frontier is the line which separates belief from unbelief. That means that it is also the line between false and true religion where cherished beliefs are challenged, contradicted or even, when necessary, condemned. With regard to the latter, the practice of *sati* in the Indian context was identified, by William Carey, as morally wrong and William Wilberforce was instrumental in the abolition of the slave trade.[380]

It is important that the Bible should be respected, in any shaping of things to come, because it is the authoritative source of our understanding of evangelism and engagement. The church's mission is about presenting the unique and universal claims of Jesus and that runs counter to the pluralist agenda. The church's mission is about calling people to repentance, faith and community relationship. We are partners in this great work in progress. Consider the challenging words of the well-known hymn:

Facing a Task Unfinished [381]

Facing a task unfinished
That drives us to our knees
A need that, undiminished
Rebukes our slothful ease
We, who rejoice to know Thee
Renew before Thy throne
The solemn pledge we owe Thee
To go and make Thee known

Where other lords beside Thee
Hold their unhindered sway
Where forces that defied Thee
Defy Thee still today
With none to heed their crying
For life, and love, and light
Unnumbered souls are dying
And pass into the night

We bear the torch that flaming

---

[380] *Sati* is the former Indian funeral custom where a widow immolated herself on her husband's pyre, or committed suicide in another fashion shortly after her husband's death.

[381] Frank Houghton, (1894-1972), *Christian Hymns*, ed. Paul E. G. Cook and Graham Harrison (Evangelical Movement of Wales, 1977).

196

Fell from the hands of those
Who gave their lives proclaiming
That Jesus died and rose
Ours is the same commission
The same glad message ours
Fired by the same ambition
To Thee we yield our powers

O Father who sustained them
O Spirit who inspired
Savior, whose love constrained them
To toil with zeal untired
From cowardice defend us
From lethargy awake!
Forth on Thine errands send us
To labor for Thy sake.

Holy Joe's

An early example of a Postmodern emergent Christian community is Holy Joe's which used to meet in a pub in Victoria, London in the 1990s. The then pastor Dave Tomlinson is the author of the provocative book *The Post-Evangelical*.[382] They had a varied program which incorporated debate, discussion, worship, Bible study, and workshops. Holy Joe's was not affiliated with any particular group or church and welcomed participation from Christian and non-Christian alike.

It was a place for people who were disillusioned with the church. It existed to reach people who were previously in churches but had ceased attending church. It was successful in reaching Postmodern people who struggled with all kinds of questions and frustrations with the institutionalized church. People at odds with evangelicalism were attracted to it. Similar projects sprang up in

---

[382] Dave Tomlinson, *The Post-Evangelical*, (London, United Kingdom: Triangle, 1995).

other places and those who found evangelicalism too constraining gravitated to them to experience a more vital faith.

Believing that Christianity is ultimately a communal faith Dave and his wife Pat started Holy Joe's at a local pub. The format was simple and the atmosphere was very relaxed. People behaved as they normally would in a pub. They drank and smoked, and they participated as much or as little as they wished, and, if they really did not like it, they just moved through to the main bar. They used to have worship evenings, which tended to be quite contemplative, with plenty of candles, symbols, and ambient music, and they had Bible study evenings where people eagerly took part in trying to understand and interpret the Scriptures.

Holy Joe's was, understandably, controversial in more than one way. Dave Tomlinson questioned the standard evangelical view of biblical inerrancy. Holy Joe's apparently did not take a clear stand on homosexuality. The "church" provided an alternative to institutionalized churches and was openly critical of them. More than one evangelical responded to Tomlinson's book with the reaction that if that was the form of things to come, they didn't want it. Although such a "church" is inevitably going to be a magnet for the disgruntled there is, nevertheless, much in Tomlinson's book that is thought-provoking, and deserves and honest engagement. And there is no doubt that many who felt there was no place for them in the regular church found in Holy Joe's a safe haven to foster their faith.[383]

Conclusion

There are some parallels with many of the Postmodern gatherings. Many of them reach out to students and often grow rapidly. Services often have worship sessions led by guitar-driven, loud bands, which is not necessarily a bad thing. There is no doubt in my mind that many in these congregations hunger for authentic

---

[383]Holy Joes does not meet at the time of writing and Dave Tomlinson is currently Anglican vicar of St. Luke's, Holloway in north London. Holy Joes has petered out but there are many similar ventures still extant.

spirituality. There is equally no doubt that many attend such places of worship for the buzz! But then the motives for attending conventional churches could also be examined and I doubt that they are always pure. If the wounded and weary and lost and lonely are gravitating to these gatherings and hearing the gospel preached that is a positive thing.

Often these churches have hard-hitting messages which are tied into contemporary issues in the public psyche, like movies etc. In the process leaders frequently share openly and honestly about their own failings and weaknesses. Some of these gatherings make every effort not to appear organized or structured as that smacks of inauthenticity. In many instances, the people who attend these gatherings are reacting to what they perceive as the ultra-conservative values of their home churches, particularly in relation to drinking alcohol, dancing and codes of dress, etc.

Does it really matter if the pastor is a young man in T-shirt and jeans? I suppose how one answers that question places one somewhere on the evangelical spectrum.

Often such gatherings dispense with pews and formal seating arrangements and opt instead for couches. They talk of the spiritual life as a journey, which is a popular perspective in Postmodern culture. Where Modernism emphasized the destination, Postmodernism puts more emphasis on the journey.

Dealing with Questions

A church that focuses on concerns in Postmodern culture will address issues such as:

- "Christians are hypocrites."

- "The Church is a cold, hierarchical institution."

- "Christians are narrow-minded."

- "Sure, I believe in God, but not your God."

- "What's the deal with Christianity's exclusive claim that Jesus is the only way to God? I don't buy it!"

- "How could a loving God send people to hell?"
- "The Bible is full of errors."

Music will play a big part, and they will use various ethnic styles ~ from bagpipes to pan flutes. The hope is that this musical effort will create an atmosphere where God's Spirit can freely move within both the musicians and worshipers.

Real Church

Postmodern churches often describe themselves as non-denominational, non-fundamentalist and non-judging. Obviously, their perception is that people around the church tend to regard the Church as split by wars into various denominations, which are essentially fundamentalist and judgmental and they are concerned not to propagate the image.

Church exists to be a healthy and celebrating family of individuals experiencing the love of God the Father together and then expressing that love to one another and to a spiritually disconnected and often emotionally hurting generation of seekers who have not yet experienced friendship with God. Our goal should be to help people move toward faith, wholeness, and spiritual maturity. Thus, we need to provide helpful ways for people to grow in authentic devotion to Christ.

We must recognize that many people today have few real friends and are lonely. There are many subcultures which are "virtually" connected (such as Gamers) but who live essentially isolated solitary lives. Many just do not know how to make good friends or be a real friend. Thus, we need to build a church where friendships are highly valued.

We need to try to communicate and teach the timeless and relevant truth of the wisdom of God and life in Christ through contemporary, creative, culturally relevant means which are attractive to a Postmodern generation of seekers, without compromising the integrity of the biblical message.

We should not be churches that are made up of only young people. We should be multi-generational and multi-ethnic communities that encourage cross-generational modeling and mentoring. Those who have experienced more of life and God have so much to give and share with those who are a little further back in the learning process.

Our goal should be to be a church which serves people not merely a church served by people. Therefore, we need to try to help people figure out who they are uniquely designed by God to be and then equip and release them as best we can to live out their God-given gifts, passions, personality, and abilities. That service may happen within the church, but it may not. There are many opportunities for gifted service within the community around us as well. We need to try to help the right people serve in the right place for the right reason at the right time.

We must recognize the reality that most people come to and mature in Christ over time through a process. Therefore, we must respect and encourage this process while demonstrating understanding and grace when progress is slow.

The Postmodern context requires a new approach to church.[384] There are thousands of churches in various parts of the world that are trying new approaches. They are attempting to reach contemporary people. These churches are seeking to interact with the Postmodern context in one or more ways. Some do so consciously, some not so consciously. Because Modernism and Postmodernism are both still powerful forces in our societies, none of these ministries reach only Postmodern people. All of them face mixed audiences, and each has a different context, which it tries to engage in its unique way.

One can admire the zeal of these churches. They are committed to shedding the less wonderful aspects of the Modern heritage, and to rediscovering biblical Christianity. They are committed to winning the lost and to becoming a community of

---

[384] Robert N. Nash, Jr., *An 8-Track Church in a CD World* (Macon, Georgia: Smyth & Helwys Publishing, 1997), 38.

believers. They are convinced that the churches in which they grew up lacked authenticity and relationship, and in this regard they are setting higher standards for themselves.

They can be admired for their creativity. Many of them are in fact reinventing themselves in their efforts to engage contemporary culture. They are writing new music and publishing new worship C.D.s. Believing that God is a creative God they are exploring artistic creativity in painting, sculpting, drama and dance.

If there is one thing we can conclude, it is that there is not just one single way to do ministry in the Postmodern era. Instead, there are many ways, even within the same cultural context.

Real Concerns

However, as already expressed, there are also a number of concerns with regard to these new churches. A primary concern is for the theology of such churches. Modernism and Postmodernism are both powerful worldviews and have tremendous impact on all the ways life is approached, including theology. In their desire to reach out to Postmodern people, some churches tend to want to minimize the differences between them and other churches. They do so in the belief that lack of unity is detrimental to the Christians testimony. In the process, they gloss over the differences, often without examining to what extent these differences might be essential.

Most of these churches refuse to enter the classical evangelical debate on inerrancy; many take no stance on creation versus evolution, and some are dabbling with ideas such as annihilationism.[385] There is also a desire to interact with certain more liberal theologians such as Lindbeck and Hauerwas, and some simply want to move beyond this division in theology.[386]

---

[385] The idea that souls condemned to the second death simply cease to exist. In this concept "hell" is simply a figure of speech.

[386] See for instance Nancey Murphey, *Beyond Liberalism & Fundamentalism - How Modern and Postmodern Philosophy set the Theological Agenda* (Valley Forge, Pennsylvania: Trinity Press, 1996).

Theologians such as D. A. Carson and Millard Erickson have expressed their concern over the direction theologians such as Donald Bloesch and Stanley Grenz are taking.[387] Many of the leaders of these churches also find much inspiration in the writings of Catholic Theologian Henri Nouwen.[388]

There is an eagerness to engage in dialogue with non-evangelical theologians, in particular liberal and Catholic theologians. There is also a broadening of the sources used in theology. This frequently includes an emphasis on narrative-shaped experience rather than propositional truths enshrined in doctrines. The sources may include, in addition to the Bible, Christian tradition, culture, and contemporary Christian experience.

A further concern is the emphasis on narrative preaching, or rather the way narrative preaching is happening. While narrative preaching is no doubt very important in the Postmodern context, and will probably become a premier form of religious communication, it is unfortunate that many preachers have a very limited understanding of what narrative preaching entails. In many situations, it seems to mean little more than sharing personal experiences or telling stories. At best, it is often limited to telling one Bible story and then extracting lessons from it which are not actually inherent in it. There seems to be general disregard for the whole story of the Bible in all its grandeur (i.e. metanarrative), and some preachers seldom demonstrate how one story, or one concept fits into the overall picture. The concern in this respect is that the concept of narrative preaching is simply not being developed to its full potential, or even to a level where it is effective in helping people develop a biblical worldview.

Another concern has to do with the degree to which these churches adapt stylistically to the culture. While the attempt to

---

[387] See e.g. Millard Erickson, *The Evangelical Left* (Grand Rapids, Michigan: Baker Book House, 1997), *Postmodernizing the Faith* (Grand Rapids, Michigan: Baker Book House, 1998), and Carson, *The Gagging of God*.

[388] See e.g. Henri Nouwen, *The Wounded Healer* (New York: Double Day, 1972) and *Creative Ministry* (New York: Double Day, 1978).

contextualize stylistically as much as possible is admirable, the question does come up: to what extent are they pursuing something that is more dictated by fashion than by meaning? Are they trying to be meaningful, or are they really just being fashionable? Knowing that few things change as quick as "what's in and what's out", this really is a question of permanence. Are the leaderships of these churches building communities that will stick together in time, or are these churches just bound together by their preferences in taste for the moment? Seeing how so many ministries reach out to young people, who are still very much in the business of growing up, this is a serious question and one which we will only be able to answer in time.

Some are also concerned about the single focus on one generation or age group that is displayed by many of these ministries. They focus on a specific target group, stylistically, for instance by using a choice of music that is particular only to that group. This brings up two questions.

First, is it possible to experience true community, as all of these ministries so greatly desire, without including multiple or all generations? Can one really understand community when one only dwells with people who are all alike?[389]

Secondly, what churches will reach out to people who have an essentially Postmodern view and experience of the world, but do not like screaming guitars or a sea of candles? Unfortunately too often churches seem to think that the Postmodern worldview is only held by that select group of young people in their twenties and early thirties. The truth of the matter is that in many places of the world in which we live, and particularly in the cities, the vast majority of our (potential) audience has a more Postmodern view of reality than we might have imagined.

While one can be thankful for the churches that reach the Goth subculture or the Grunge scene etc., there is an obvious need for more churches that target people in mainstream culture.

---

[389] See e.g. Leighton G. Ford and Jim Denney, *The Power of Story - Rediscovering the Oldest, Most Natural Way to Reach People for Christ* (Colorado Springs: NavPress, 1994).

A connected concern is that, in order to reach young people, many ministries set themselves up near college-campuses. This gives them access to large amounts of people that fit their target profile. For that group, they then provide a unique church experience. The down-side of their chosen location, however, is that many of these people will move on after graduation. This leads to two questions. What does that do to the church itself? But more importantly perhaps, is the question how will the individual cope with leaving. Having enjoyed such a unique experience they are not very likely to find a church that will be what they are looking for. While this question does not in any way invalidate these ministries, it does reveal the fact that churches that are actively and successfully ministering to Postmodern people are still few and far between.

In conclusion, it can be said that the emergence of these churches is a hopeful sign. God will not leave himself without a witness in the Postmodern era. Nevertheless, there is reason to be concerned about the theological and practical questions some of these churches face. Furthermore, they are relatively few, although more and more are emerging. Lastly, it is too early to tell what type of impact these churches will make.

The world is changing. Everything is being redefined. Many Christians find themselves surprised, and perhaps even discouraged, by the developments in the world. Amidst this upheaval one can feel insecure, and one might like to hold on to that which is familiar. Sometimes there is temptation to defend tooth and nail that, which is now passing, in the vain hope that it will last.

This transition from Modernism to Postmodernism can seem like a slow-motion earthquake. It is as if history finds itself on the edge of two enormous tectonic plates that are slipping and sliding, bumping and grinding. Until the earthquake ends, there is little certainty regarding what things will look like.

While this may be scary, it is also very exciting. Christians at the start of the third millennium have the privilege of being part of a conversation about the nature of things that is characterized by profoundness and a search for truth. This is exciting because this conversation is opening our eyes to some new things, and it creates

205

the opportunity to discover that the Christian faith is still relevant and applicable in this new context.

The Postmodern world challenges Christians in a number of ways. The Postmodern world challenges them to familiarize themselves with it. While it is not "home" to Christians, it is their residence for the moment. It is the location of the church's operations. In becoming familiar with the Postmodern world, it is important that Christians not allow themselves to be motivated by fear or disgust, but by love, much like the Savior was when he came into the world. The Postmodern world challenges Christians to understand people where they are at. Can they sense their hopelessness? Are they in touch with their desire to be free? Can they hear their heart-cry? The Postmodern world challenges them to leave behind their pet notions and cheap excuses and to get their hands dirty.

The Postmodern world challenges them to reconsider the way they see the world. It challenges them to let go of Modern presuppositions. It challenges the understanding of truth. It challenges them to assign rationalism its proper place, allowing proper room for the emotions and spirituality of the human being.

The Postmodern world challenges them to tell their story and tell it well. Ours is a grand and powerful story that encompasses all of reality, and which captures every element of the human existence. While there are many other stories out there, ours stands out in many ways. In our story, people meet Jesus, who is the image of the invisible God (Colossians 1:15). Our story provides meaning, morality and mission.

The Postmodern world challenges Christians and churches everywhere to be the best community of faith they can be. In a world where people are more and more alienated by distance, technology and broken relationships, and where people find their identity by being part of groups, people are hungry and needy for community. The Postmodern world challenges the church to be a community of healing to all.

The Postmodern world challenges Christians to live lives of vital spirituality. With its openness to the supernatural, the Christian claim of spirituality is not at odds with the Postmodern world. The Postmodern world has a hunger for experience of the supernatural. In the Christian community and worship, through its story and its prayers, Postmodern people can, in fact, encounter the divine.

The Postmodern world challenges Christians to become a personal demonstration of their story. It challenges them to be authentic and sincere. It challenges them to live their morals rather than just preach them.

The Postmodern world challenges every interest group to recognize its vested interests, and to develop a healthy sense of self-critique. Where Modern man regarded the world from his own position, from the inside out, Postmodern man looks at himself from other positions, from the outside in. The Postmodern world challenges everyone to re-examine themselves, to look from the outside in.

The Postmodern world challenges everyone to contribute to the community at large. It encourages people to think globally and act locally. It invites everyone to the discussion table. Christians can participate in the conversation, as long as they realize that they cannot regulate it, or dictate the outcome. The Postmodern world is intimately familiar with past Christian partnership with various forms of oppression. With those memories in mind, it invites Christians to serve a world in need, and it observes them, to see if they will rise to the challenge.

Much in the Postmodern world is difficult to like. Its relative view of truth, lack of morality, and the way in which it seeks to limit the Christian role in society are just a few examples. But the world is becoming increasingly Postmodern, and Jesus sends his disciples to it, regardless of the circumstances.

To gather the harvest, disciples the world over must now learn how to harvest in the Postmodern era. This requires them to understand Postmodernism without becoming Postmodernist. This can be done, and many are already showing the way

Other Books by Kieran Beville

JOURNEY WITH JESUS THROUGH THE MESSAGE OF MARK

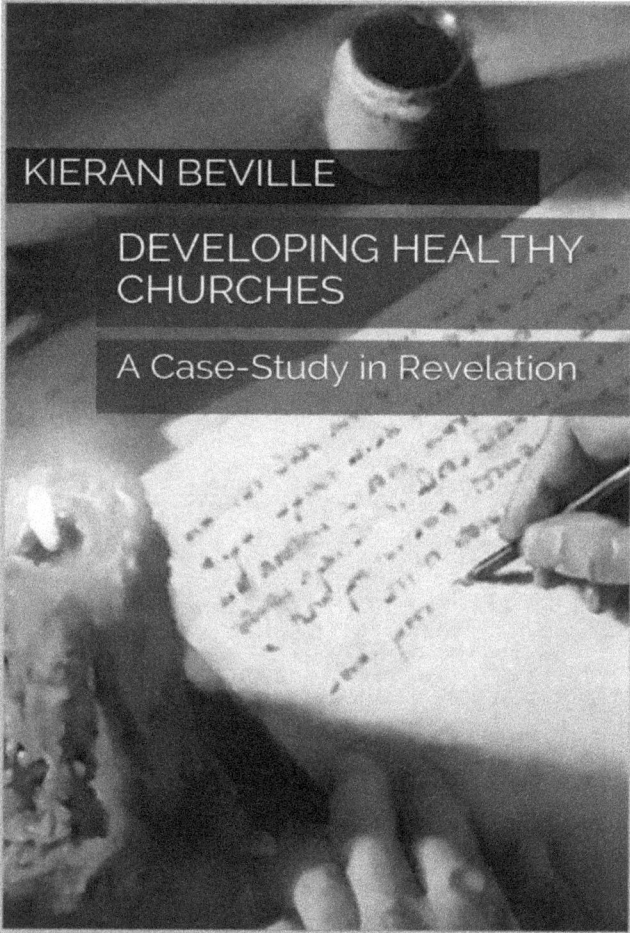

DYING TO KILL: A Christian Perspective on Euthanasia and Assisted Suicide

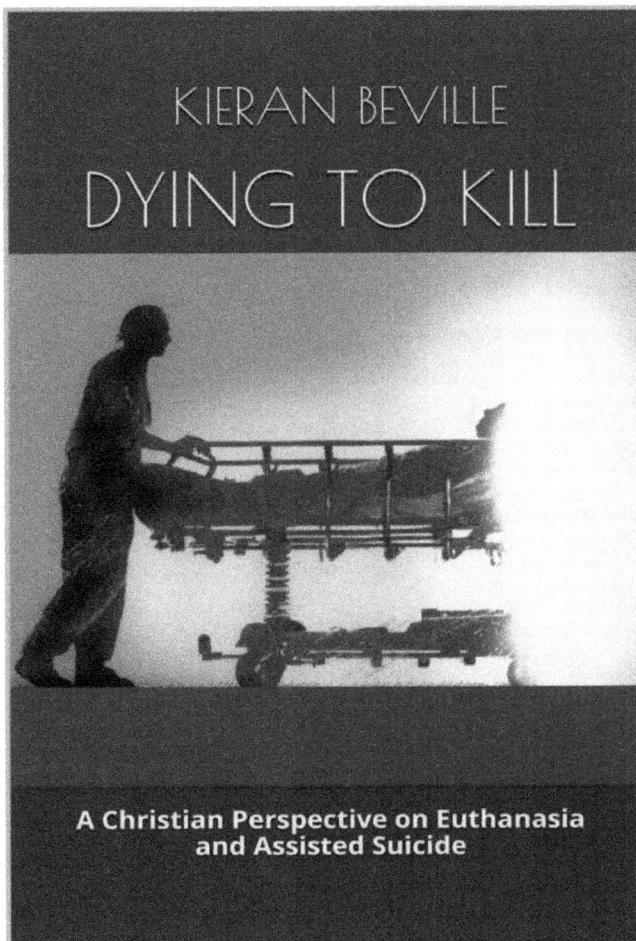

SELECT BIBLIOGRAPHY

Allen, Diogenes. *Christian Belief in a Postmodern World - The Full Wealth of Conviction*, (Louisville, Kentucky: Westminster/John Knox Press, 1989).

Allen, Ronald J., Barbara Shires Blaisdell and Scott Black Johnston. *Theology for Preaching -Authority, Truth and Knowledge of God in a Postmodern Ethos*, (Nashville, Tennessee: Abbingdon Press, 1997).

Anderson, Walter Truett. *Reality Isn't What It Used To Be*, (New York: Harper Collins Publishers, 1992).

--- ed. *The Truth About The Truth*, (New York, Tarcher/Putnam Books, 1995).

Babin, Pierre and Mercedes Iannone. *The New Ear in Religious Communication*. (Minneapolis, Minnesota: Fortress Press, 1991).

Barrett, David. "Status of Global Missions, 1996, in Context of the 20th and 21st Centuries", *International Bulletin of Missionary Research*, January 1996.

Barna, George. *The Invisible Generation: Baby Busters*, (Glendale, California: Barna Research Group, 1992).

---*The Second Coming of the Church - a Blueprint for Survival*, (Nashville, Tennessee: Word Publishing, 1998).

Beaudoin, Tom. *Virtual Faith*, (San Francisco: Jossey-Bass Publishers, 1998).

Bellah, Robert. *The Good Society*, (New York: Vintage, 1991).

Beville, Kieran. *Preaching Christ in a Postmodern Culture*, (Cambridge Scholar's Press, 2010).

Boomerhsine, Thomas. *Story Journey - An Invitation To The Gospel as Story Telling*, (Nashville, Tennessee: Abingdon Press, 1988).

Bosch, David J. *Believing in the Future - Toward a Missiology of Western Culture*, (Valley Forge, Pennsylvania: Trinity Press International, 1995).

Bottum, J. "Christians and PostModerns" *First Things*, 40 (Feb., 1994).

Bradford, Lawrence J. and Claire Raines. *Twenty Something - Managing and Motivating Today's New Workforce*, (Denver, Colorado: Merrill-Alexander Publishing, 1992).

Bultmann, Rudolf. "Pistueo", in *Theological Dictionary of the New Testament*, abridged ed., (Grand Rapids, Michigan: Eerdmans, 1985).

Burge, Gary M. "Are Evangelicals Missing God at Church?" *Christianity Today*, (October 6, 1997).

Carson, D. A. *The Gagging of God - Christianity Confronts Pluralism*, (Grand Rapids, Michigan: Zondervan, 1996).

Celek, Tim and Dieter Zander. *Inside the Soul Of a New Generation – Insights and Strategies for Reaching Busters*, (Grand Rapids, Michigan: Zondervan Publishing House, 1996).

Clapp, Rodney. *A Peculiar People - The Church in a Post-Christian Society*, (Downer's Grove, Illinois: InterVarsity press, 1996).

Coupland, Douglas. *Life After God*, (New York: Pocket Books, 1994).

Derrida, Jacques. Translated by Gayatri Chakravorty Spivak, *Of Grammatology*, (Maryland, Baltimore: John Hopkins University Press, 1967).

Dockery, David S., ed. *The Challenge of Postmodernism - An Evangelical Engagement*, (Wheaton: Illinois: Bridgepoint, 1995).

Edwards, Tamala. "Get Thee to a Monastery." *TIME* (U.S. edition, 3 August 1998).

Erickson, Millard J. *The Evangelical Left*, (Grand Rapids, Michigan: Baker Book House Publishing Company, 1997).

---*Postmodernizing the Faith*, (Grand Rapids, Michigan: Baker Book House, 1998).

Fitzgerald, Dave. "The Future of Belief", (*First Things*, 63 May 1996).

Ford, Kevin J. "My Generation." *Intervarsity*, winter, 1994-95.

---*Jesus For a New Generation - Putting the Gospel in the Language of X'ers.* (Downers Grove, Illinois: Intervarsity Press, 1995).

---*LEADERSHIP* Journal, (Fall 1996, Vol. XVII, No. 4).

Ford, Leighton and Jim Denney. *The Power of Story - Rediscovering the Oldest, Most Natural Way to reach People for Christ*, (Colorado Springs, Colorado: NavPress, 1994).

Frank, Anne. *Anne Frank - The Diary of a Young Girl*, trans. B.M. Mooyaart-(Doubleday. New York: Doubleday, 1967).

Frost, Michael and Alan Hirsch. *The Shaping of Things to Come*, (Massachusetts: USA, Hendrickson, and Australia: Strand Publishing, 2003).

Gergen, Kenneth J. *The Saturated Self*, (New York: Basic Books, 1991).

Gerhart, Mary. "Generic Competence in Biblical Hermeneutics", *Semeia* 43 (1988).

Greig, Gary S. and Kevin Springer. eds. *The Kingdom and the Power*. Ventura, (California: Regal Books, 1993).

Grenz, Stanley J. *A Primer on Postmodernism*, (Grand Rapids, Michigan: Eerdmans Publishing Company, 1995).

Groothuis, Douglas. "Facing the Challenge of Postmodernism", *To Everyone and Answer: A Case for the Christian Worldview*, Francis Beckwith, William Lane Craig and J. P. Moreland eds. (Downers Grove, Illinois: IVP, 2004).

Guinness, Os. *Dining with the Devil*, (Grand Rapids: Baker, 1993).

Hahn, Todd and David Verhaagen. *Reckless Hope - Understanding and Reaching Baby Busters*, (Grand Rapids, Michigan: Baker Book House, 1996).

Halter, Hugh and Matt Smay. *The Tangible Kingdom*, (San Francisco: CA, Jossey-Bass, 2008).

Hauerwas, Stanley. "Preaching as Though We Had Enemies", *First Things 53*, (May 1995).

Hesselgrave, David J. and Edgar Rommen. *Contextualization*, (Grand Rapids, Michigan: Baker Book House, 1992).

--- *Communicating Christ Cross-Culturally - An Introduction to Missionary Communication*, (2d ed., Grand Rapids, Michigan: Zondervan, 1991).

Hunter, George III. *How to Reach Secular People*, (Nashville, Tennessee: Abingdon Press, 1992).

--- *Church for the Unchurched* (Nashville, Tennessee: Abingdon Press, 1996).

Johns, Jackie David. "Pentecostalism and the Postmodern Worldview" (*Journal of Pentecostal Theology 7*, 1995).

Kallenberg, Brad J. "Conversion Converted: A Postmodern Formulation of the Doctrine of Conversion", (*Evangelical Quarterly 67:4*, 1995).

Kennedy, D. James. *Evangelism Explosion*, (Wheaton, Illinois: Tyndale House Publishers, 1970).

Knight, Henry H., III. *A Future for Truth - Evangelical Theology in a Postmodern World*, (Nashville, Tennessee: Abbingdon Press, 1997).

Lindbeck, George A. *The Nature of Doctrine*, (Philadelphia, Pennsylvania: Westminster Press, 1984).

Long, Jimmy. *Generation Hope - A Strategy for Reaching the Postmodern Generation*, (Downers Grove, Illinois: InterVarsity Press, 1997).

Lyotard, Jean-Francois. (Translated by Geoff Bennington and Brian Massumi) *The Postmodern Condition - a Report on Knowledge.*, (Minneapolis, Minnesota: University of Minnesota Press, 1984).

Mahedy, William, and Janet Bernardi. *A Generation Alone - X'ers Making a Place in the World*, (Downers Grove, Illinois: IVP Press, 1994).

McCallum, Dennis, ed. *The Death of Truth*, (Minneapolis, Minnesota: Bethany Book Publishers, 1996).

McDowell, Josh. *Evidence that Demands a Verdict*, (San Bernardino, California: Here's Life Publishers, 1972).

McGrath, Alistair. *A Passion for Truth - The Intellectual Coherence of Evangelicalism*, (Downers Grove, Illinois: Intervarsity Press, 1996).

McLaren, Brian D. *Reinventing Your Church*, (Grand Rapids, Michigan: Zondervan, 1998).

--- *Finding Faith*, (Grand Rapids, Michigan: Zondervan, 1999).

Mahedy, William and Janet Bernardi. *A Generation Alone - X'ers Making a Place in the World*, (Downers Grove, Illinois: IVP Press, 1994).

Middleton, J. Richard and Brian J. Walsh. *Truth is Stranger Than It Used to Be*, (Downers Grove, Illinois: Intervarsity Press, 1995).

Migliore, Daniel L. *Faith Seeking Understanding: An Introduction to Christian Theology*, (Grand Rapids, Michigan: Eerdmans, 1996).

Miller, Dennis. *Reinventing American Protestantism: Christianity in the New Millennium*, (University of California Press, 1997).

Moore, Scott H. "Era and Epoch, Epoch and Era: Christian Intellectuals in the Postmodern Turn", (*Christian Scholar's Review*, Volume XXVI, Number 2, Winter 1996).

Morgan, Timothy C. "The Alpha Brits are Coming" *Christianity Today*, February 9, 1998 Vol. 42, No. 2.

Murphey, Nancy. *Beyond Liberalism & Fundamentalism - How Modern and Postmodern Philosophy Set The Theological Agenda*, (Rockwell Lecture Series. Valley Forge, Pennsylvania: Trinity Press, 1996).

Nash, Robert N., Jr. *An 8-Track Church in a CD World*, (Macon, Georgia: Smyth & Helwys Publishing, 1997).

Newbigin, Lesslie. *The Gospel in a Pluralist Society*, (Grand Rapids, Michigan: Eerdmans Publishing Company, 1989).

--- *Proper Confidence: Faith, Doubt and Certainty in Christian Discipleship*, (Grand Rapids Michigan: Eerdmans, 1995).

Niebuhr, H. Richard. *Christ and Culture*, (New York: Harper and Row, 1951).

Nietzche, Friedrich. *Thus Spoke Zarathustra*, (New York: Penguin Books, 1954).

Nouwen, Henri J.M. *The Wounded Healer*, (New York: Doubleday,   1979).
--- *Creative Ministry*, (New York: Doubleday, 1971).

Oden, Thomas C. *Between Two Worlds - Notes on the Death of Modernity in America and Russia*, (Downers Grove, Illinois: Intervarsity Press, 1992).

After Modernity... What? Agenda For Theology, (Grand Rapids, Michigan: Zondervan Publishing House, 1992).

--- *Pastoral Theology,* (San Francisco: Harper and Row, 1982).

Osborn, Lawrence. "Collision Crossroads: The Intersection of Modern Western Culture with the Christian Gospel", *The Gospel and Culture,* ed. J. Flett. Auckland, (The DeepSight Trust, 1998).

Padgett, Alan. "Christianity and Postmodernity", *(Christian Scholar's Review,* Volume XXVI, Number 2, Winter 1996), Special Issue: *Christianity and Postmodernity.*

Rabey, Steve. "Church in Action", *(Christianity Today,* November 11, 1996, Vol. 40, No. 13).

Robertson, Pat. *Turning Tide,* (Dallas, Texas: Word, 1996).

Sandel, Michael. "America's Search for a New Public Philosophy", *(Atlantic Monthly,* March 1996).

Sampson, Philip, Vinay Samuel and Chris Sugden, eds. *Faith and Modernity,* (Oxford, United Kingdom: Regnum Books, 1994).

Sine, Tom. *Cease Fire - Searching for Sanity in America's Culture Wars,* (Grand Rapids, Michigan: William B. Eerdmans Publishing House, 1995).

Sjogren, Steve. *Conspiracy Of Kindness,* (Ann Arbor, Michigan: Servant Publication: 1993).

Slaughter, Michael. *Out on the Edge: A Wake-Up Call for Church Leaders on the Edge of the Media Reformation,* (Nashville, Tennessee: Abingdon Press, 1998).

Stafford, Tim. "God's Missionary to Us", *(Christianity Today,* 40, December 9, 1996).

Tapia, Andros. "Reaching the First Post Christian Generation", *(Christianity Today* September 12, 1994).

Thiselton, Anthony C. *Interpreting God and the Postmodern Self On Meaning, Manipulation and Promise,* (Grand Rapids, Michigan: Eerdmans Publishing Company, 1995).

Tomlinson, Dave. *The Post-Evangelical,* (London, UK: Triangle, 1995).

Toulmin, Stephen. *Cosmopolis,* (Chicago, Illinois: Inversity of Chicago Press, 1990).

Tozer, A. W. *The Root of the Righteous,* (Harrisburgh, PA: Christian Publications, 1955).

Van Rheenen, Gailyn "Modern and Postmodern Syncretism in Theology and Missions", *The Holy Spirit and Mission Dynamics,* ed. C. Douglas McConnell, (Pasadena: Wm. Carey, 1997).

Veith, Gene Edward, Jr. *Postmodern Times - A Christian Guide to Contemporary Thought and Culture,* (Wheaton, Illinois: Crossway Books, 1994).

Waugh, Patricia. *Postmodernism: A Reader,* (London: Edward Arnold, 1992).

Ward, Graham. "Introduction: 'Where We Stand'," in *The Blackwell Companion to Postmodern Theology,* ed. Graham Ward, (Oxford and Malden, Mass.: Blackwell Publishers, 2001).

Wells, David F. *God in the Wasteland: The Reality of Truth in a World of Fading Dreams,* (Wm. B. Eerdmans, Grand Rapids: Michigan, and Inter-Varsity Press, Leicester: England, 1994).

Willard, Dallas. *The Divine Conspiracy - Rediscovering Our Hidden Life in God,* (San Francisco, California: Harper, 1998).

Wright, Eric E. *A Practical Theology of Missions: Dispelling the Mystery; Recovering the Passion,* (DayOne, UK, 2010).

Yancey, Philip. *What's so Amazing About Grace?* (Grand Rapids, Michigan: Zondervan Publishing House, 1997).

Yates, T. *Christian Mission in the Twentieth Century,* (Cambridge Universtity Press, 1994).

Zander, Dieter. "Reaching the Busters: One Church's Experience", (*Lead On,* spring 1994).

www.ingramcontent.com/pod-product-compliance
Lightning Source LLC
Chambersburg PA
CBHW031835090426
42741CB00005B/252

9 780692 637685